Feast of Lupercal ?

William Shakespeare's

Making Sense of Julius Caesar!

A Students Guide to Shakespeare's Play

Includes Study Guide, Biography, and Modern Retelling

BookCaps™ Study Guides

www.bookcaps.com

Cover Image © pcanzo - Fotolia.com

Table of Contents

Study Guide

Historical Context

Shakespeare's Julius Caesar takes place in Rome around 44 B.C. At that time, the Roman Empire was at its largest, and, as a result, political division was occurring throughout the country. Many men tried to step up and unify Rome, but only Julius Caesar came close to being successful. Several members of the Roman aristocracy, fearing Caesar would become a tyrant, plotted to assassinate him. Instead of bringing peace to Rome, however, Caesar's death fueled a bloody civil war.

Shakespeare's play is a dramatized version of these historical events, focusing specifically on the height of Caesar's power and popularity, his assassination by the political conspirators, and the beginning of the civil war. Most scholars believe that Shakespeare got his historical information from Plutarch's The Life of Julius Caesar, a well-known and trusted biography written during the Greek and Roman times, and later translated into English.

Julius Caesar was likely performed sometime between 1599 and 1601 at Shakespeare's Globe Theatre. The official text, however, was not published until 1623, in the first compilation released after Shakespeare's death. The original manuscript doesn't exist, and it is likely that the play was based off the Theatre manuscripts. Because the play was released at the height of Shakespeare's popularity and resonated with the political turmoil of the time, it became one of his most famous historical tragedies. While many of his other plays went in and out of style throughout the years, Julius Caesar has remained consistently popular.

Shakespeare himself was born in 1564 to middle-class parents in England. He received limited schooling and married in 1582 to an older woman. In 1590, Shakespeare left his family and moved to London to start his career, and soon became immensely successful. At the height of his career, he helped build the Globe Theatre to accommodate the popularity of his plays. Because of the high demand for new entertainment, Shakespeare wrote a total of 37 known plays and numerous poems. Julius Caesar was likely the first play performed at the Globe Theatre.

After his death in 1616, he quickly became known as England's best playwright and remains highly influential to this day. Because so many facts about Shakespeare's life are unknown, there are some who think that Shakespeare was a woman, or that someone else actually wrote the plays. However, there is no hard evidence to back these conspiracies up. While people may always argue about Shakespeare's true identity, his plays, and especially Julius Caesar, have become an indispensable part of literary history.

Plot Summary

official in ancient Rome chosen by plebeians to protect their interests.

Act one opens on the streets of Rome. Many of the lower-class workers are roaming around the streets. Two Tribunes, Flavius and Marullus, question two citizens to find out what is going on. It turns out that Caesar has defeated his rival, Pompey, in battle, and the citizens are waiting to see the triumphant parade. Flavius and Marullus scatter the groups of workers and remark that Caesar's popularity has become too strong. They begin to take down the decorations marking Caesar's statues.

Meanwhile, Caesar and the rest of the parade enter. A Soothsayer calls out to Caesar, telling him to beware the "ides of March" (March 15th). Caesar ignores the Soothsayer and continues on his way. Caesar exits, leaving Brutus and Cassius behind on the stage. Cassius wishes to talk to Brutus and notes that he has not seemed like himself lately. Brutus admits that he has been troubled, and Cassius expresses dissatisfaction with Caesar's rise in power, and fears that he will be crowned any day. Offstage, three shouts from the crowd are heard.

Caesar comes back, remarking to Mark Antony, his second-hand man, that he does not trust Cassius. Brutus and Cassius ask Casca, a politician, what the shouts were for. Casca reveals that Mark Antony offered Caesar a crown three times, and Caesar refused each time, although he looked as if he truly wanted to take it. After the third time, he collapsed in a shaking fit. Everyone exits the stage but Cassius, who plots to bring Brutus to his side by forging letters from citizens for Brutus and against Caesar.

That night there is a massive storm and many strange occurrences. Cassius wanders the streets to meet with other conspirators who want to kill Caesar. They head towards Brutus' house to convince him to join their cause. Brutus is alone in his garden, having received the letters, which he believes to be from concerned Romans. Cassius and several other conspirators show up, and Brutus, swayed by the letters, joins their cause.

They plan to kill Caesar that morning at the Senate, before they can give him a crown. Cassius thinks they should also kill Antony because of his loyalty to Caesar, but Brutus disagrees. After the group is gone, Portia, Brutus' wife, begs him to confide in her.

power of wife / love ??

That morning, Caesar is planning on heading to the Senate, but his wife, Calphurnia, urges him not to go. She has had a premonition of his death and heeds the bad omens of the night before. One of the conspirators convinces Caesar not to heed the foolish fears of a woman, and Caesar heads outside.

— views on women

On the way to the Senate, the Soothsayer again reminds Caesar to beware and is once again dismissed. A man named Artemidorus, foreseeing the evil intent of the conspirators, tries to give Caesar a letter of warning, but Caesar won't take it. Inside at the Senate meeting, the conspirators circle Caesar and stab him, Brutus last. When Caesar realizes that his most trusted friend, Brutus, betrayed him, he gives in to his death. They bathe their hands and swords in Caesar's blood, when Mark Antony comes in. Antony says he will follow Brutus if he gives a good reason for Caesar's death, and Brutus says he will at Caesar's funeral.

They take the body out to the market, and Brutus calmly tells the crowd that he killed Caesar for fear he would become a tyrant. The crowd agrees with him, and Brutus leaves. Next, Antony comes up and appeals to the crowd emotionally, reading them Caesar's will which states they have all been given money, and the crowd turns into an angry mob. They decide to kill the conspirators, and scour the streets. They mistakenly kill an innocent poet named Cinna just for sharing a name with one of the conspirators.

At Caesar's house, Octavius, Caesar's named heir, Mark Antony, and Lepidus plan to raise and army. Brutus and Cassius have been driven from the city and are gathering their power outside.

Outside the city, Brutus and Cassius argue about bribery and the future of Rome. They reconcile, and Brutus admits that he is grieving over Portia's suicide. They plan to battle the next morning, and try to get some rest. In Brutus' tent that night, Caesar's ghost appears and tells Brutus that he will see him on the battlefield.

Octavius and Antony head towards Brutus and Cassius with their army. Octavius is already asserting his role as the next Caesar, as he refuses to listen to Antony's orders. The generals meet on the battlefield to exchange insults, and the battle begins. Cassius' men flee, while Brutus' are winning. When Cassius believes his best friend, Titinius, to be captured, he kills himself. Brutus, heartbroken, battles again the next day. When they have lost, Brutus also kills himself. Octavius and Mark Antony, upon finding Brutus' corpse, declare him a true Roman because instead of killing Caesar for greed and envy, he did it for the good of Rome.

Themes

Fate

Many of the conflicts in Julius Caesar revolve around the concept of fate. Some characters, such as Caesar himself, realize that some things cannot be prevented. When Caesar is going to leave his house, he notes that everybody dies and that it does no good to run from death. Other characters, such as Cassius, do not want to believe in fate. Cassius, by killing Caesar, seeks to change his fate by making himself famous throughout history. Ultimately, however, Shakespeare does not clearly state whether or not fate in his story is real, but rather balances the ideas of fate and free will.

Misinterpretation of Signs

Part of what makes Julius Caesar a tragedy is the constant misinterpretation of signs and symbols. Every character interprets the various bad omens in the story based on their own wishes. Cassius, for instance, takes the storm, and its strange occurrences to be proof that Caesar's rise to power is causing unrest. However, based on the end of the play, the bad omens were most likely foreshadowing what would come after Caesar's death. Certain characters do interpret the signs right, Calphurnia, for instance, interprets her dream to mean Caesar's death. Decius, to convince Caesar to leave, gives him the interpretation Caesar wishes to hear, and leads Caesar to his death.

The Power of Persona

Caesar's power over the Roman Empire is based entirely on his persona, his public image, rather than the man himself. Cassius assumes that, because Caesar is weak of body, he will be easy to overthrow. He does not realize, however, the extent to which Caesar's name and the connotations that go along with it hold enormous power. At the end of the play, when Octavius Caesar rebukes Antony's orders and establishes himself as the center of command, Antony begins referring to Octavius as Caesar. Thus, even though Julius Caesar died, his persona lived on in the form of his name.

The Tragic Hero

Although the play is named after Julius Caesar, it is debatable whether or not Caesar is actually the tragic hero. On one hand, Caesar directs the action of the other characters, forcing them to act because of his rise to power. He also refers to himself as the "northern star" and his death is certainly noble. On the other hand, Caesar only appears briefly in the play, and does not possess near as many lines as Brutus. Brutus, as the protagonist, is mourned after his death by the reader and is even recognized as a tragic hero by Octavius and Antony. While there is much debate over who is the "true" tragic hero, Brutus' status as the protagonist and more emotional death point to him being the tragic hero of the story.

Patriotism

Julius Caesar is primed to take control of Rome when it has become so large it has lost its purpose. Thus it is no surprise that many of the characters in the play have different views on what is means to be a true Roman. Brutus is the most obvious example of a true Roman and is even recognized by his enemies as being such. They praise him for putting the needs of his country above everything else, and, even though he assassinated Caesar, his motives gave him more honor than the other conspirators.

Betrayal and Revenge

The most famous betrayal in Julius Caesar occurs when Brutus, one of Caesar's best friends, stabs in him the back. When Caesar sees that even Brutus has betrayed him, he accepts his death. Brutus' actions, however, do not go unpunished. He is haunted by Caesar's ghost, the physical manifestation of his betrayal to the man, until his own tragic death. Brutus' and the other conspirator's private betrayal against Caesar the man are justified by the common good, but Shakespeare hints that is not an excuse by having Caesar's ghost haunt Brutus and Cassius.

Manipulation

The majority of the characters in Julius Caesar use manipulation or persuasion to get what they want. Perhaps the most manipulative character in the play is Cassius, who forges letters falsely denouncing Caesar and leaves them for Brutus to read. Antony purposefully manipulates the crowd at Caesar's funeral through clever words and emotional appeals, saying one thing but putting the oppose idea in his speech to incite riot. Because Brutus is not skilled at manipulation, he rather attempts to view things rationally, in the end he ultimately dies.

The Supernatural

Like many of Shakespeare's plays, the supernatural has a strong presence throughout and helps aid in the resolution of the plot. The night before Caesar is assassinated, many strange sights are seen. Dead men are seen walking, men are on fire but do not burn, etc. These are taken as omens by the characters, who interpret the signs as they want. The most blatant case of the supernatural is the ghost of Julius Caesar who appears to Brutus twice. Because of Caesar's direct interference from the other side of the grave, Brutus kills himself after losing the battle.

Fear

All the conspirators who kill Caesar are, to some extent, motivated by fear. Brutus fears that Caesar will become a tyrant; Cassius fears he will never receive recognition or fame. Caesar himself is perhaps the only character who does not succumb to fear. Even though, because of many signs and warnings, he is aware that there is danger to his person, he consciously chooses not to succumb to fear.

Masculinity

The masculine versus feminine sides, although not of central importance, run through the entirety of the play. Masculinity is seen as having the public self and is embodied in the sort of thinking Brutus acts on. He ignores his personal feelings and acts on the good of Rome. The female characters of the play, on the other hand, represent the private, feminine self. Caesar, especially, is prone to analysis. Cassius views Caesar as not being able to rule because his body is weak. He has seizures, gets sick, and asks for help. These are all feminine traits. However, Caesar's powerful public persona is overwhelmingly masculine, and he deliberately chooses to ignore his wife's pleas (his feminine side), which ultimately leads to his death.

Characters

Julius Caesar

Although Julius Caesar is the namesake of the play, he is only present in three scenes. Despite this, his dominant personality and public persona are highly present throughout. He carries himself with importance and describes himself as "the northern star", always constant and steady. He chooses not to believe in signs and omens, putting his personal needs last before the needs of the people. Even after his death, he remains fixed in the minds of the characters, and his ghost continues to haunt Brutus until his eventual death.

Calphurnia

The wife of Julius Caesar, Calphurnia acts as Caesar's private, inner guide. The night before Caesar's death, Calphurnia is plagued by nightmares of people bathing themselves in a fountain of Caesar's blood. She predicts his death, and begs him the next day not to go to the Senate. By standing up for her beliefs proves her to be worthy of a man like Julius Caesar. Because Caesar doesn't listen to Calphurnia and her warnings, it ends in his eventual death.

Brutus

The true protagonist of the play, Brutus is a well-loved Roman citizen. He is torn between his inner and outer self, which causes him to struggle greatly. On one hand, he is Caesar's close friend and has a strong respect, even love, for the man. However, he believes Caesar to be capable of great evil because of his ambition. He fears that, in Caesar's reign, Rome will cease to be a democracy, and puts his love of Rome above his personal feelings for Caesar. Because of his rational nature and inability to manipulate, however, he fails to sway the people in his opinion and dies a noble death after the battle.

Portia

Brutus' wife, Portia is only present for one scene in the play, yet proves herself to be an admirable and worthy woman. After Brutus joins the conspirators, Portia begs him several times to be allowed into his confidence. When her strength and conviction alone do not convince him to confide in her, she cites her father and brother as evidence of her honor and strength. Brutus acknowledges that he is not worthy of such a woman and agrees to confide in her. Portia, as Brutus' private self, displays correct foreshadowing of events when she kills herself, knowing that Brutus will die, as well.

Cassius

Cassius is one of Brutus' close friends, and the central conspirator against Caesar. While Brutus goes against Caesar for the good of Rome, Cassius is a conspirator because he believes all the glory should not be given to one man. He questions why Caesar is better than everyone else, and why he should get so much glory. Cassius also wants to kill Antony, while Brutus believes that to be unnecessary bloodshed. True to his less-than-noble nature, Cassius' death was not as noble as Brutus'. He dies do to a misunderstanding and is too cowardly to kill himself, having his slave do the deed for him.

Mark Antony

Mark Antony is Caesar's right-hand man and the primary reason for the public backlash against Brutus and Cassius after Julius Caesar's death. After Caesar's death, Mark Antony swears loyalty to Brutus and the other conspirators, shaking their hands. When they are gone, however, he reveals that he will stop at nothing to exact revenge for Caesar's death. Antony manipulates the crowd at Caesar's funeral, saying that Brutus and Cassius are honorable men, yet lamenting at the stab wounds caused by them on Caesar's body, turning the crowd into an angry mob.

Octavius

Caesar's appointed son and heir, Octavius arrives in the city after Caesar's death. He immediately joins forces with Antony in order to go up against Brutus and Cassius. While Octavius' character is not shown enough to see great depth, he is primed to replace Caesar as the next ruler of Rome. On the battlefield, Octavius refuses to follow Antony's orders, and, from then on, Antony refers to him as Caesar. This shows that the name Caesar has gone from a mere name to a title of ruler, which Octavius stands to inherit.

The Conspirators

Other than Brutus and Cassius, there are many conspirators against Caesar. They include Casca, Trebonius, Ligarus, Decius, Metellus, and Cinna. While their true motives for killing Caesar are not explicitly known, it is hinted by Antony at the end of the play that only Brutus' motives were pure and that the others were motivated by greed, envy, and personal fear. The conspirators work together to manipulate others into joining their cause and Decius is the one who convinces Caesar to leave the morning of the Senate meeting.

The Politicians

While they do not take an active part in the conspiracy, a few of the politicians in the senate support the conspirators in their cause. The politicians seen in the play are Cicero, Publius and Lena. Lena realizes what the conspirators are going to do and wishes Cassius luck in his endeavor, causing Cassius to believe that Lena is going to betray them. Lena, however, talks to Caesar normally and stands back during the murder. Publius, another senator flees the scene for fear of being associated with the conspirators. Mark Antony and Octavius, after Caesar's death, execute a hundred Senators, showing that, even though they did not take active part in the murder they were still partially responsible.

The Tribunes

Present in the very beginning of the play, the two Tribunes are Flavius and Marullus. They question the commoners about the parade and scatter the crowds awaiting Caesar's arrival. They are the first to acknowledge fear of Caesar's growing popularity, and bring to light the potential corruption that could come along with that sort of power. They are arrested for taking down decorations off of Caesar's statues.

The Soothsayer

Never named, the Soothsayer represents the supernatural and also the hands of fate. He attempts to prevent Caesar's fate by warning him of the "ides of March" and the danger in that day, but Caesar ignores his warnings. The Soothsayer briefly talks to Portia, and reveals that he does not know the exact nature of the danger Caesar is in and does not believe that Caesar will listen to him, but will warn him anyway.

Artemidorus

Not much is known about Artemidorus besides the fact that he clearly sees the intentions of the conspirators and believes that Caesar should be the ruler of Rome. Artemidorus writes Caesar a letter detailing why he should not trust those around him and attempts to give the letter to Caesar on the morning of his death disguised as a petition. Caesar refuses to read the letter, stating that his personal matters will be dealt with after those of the common good.

Cinna the Poet

Cinna the poet is an unfortunate man who happens to share the same name as Cinna the conspirator. He is killed by the enraged mob, even though he is innocent of conspiracy, because they mistake his identity for Cinna the traitor. His death shows that the mob does not listen to reason, and that they can commit terrible acts in the name of revenge.

The Soldiers

Lucilius and Titinius are the two main soldiers in the last half of the play. Lucilius is Brutus' general and Titinius Cassius'. Both are extremely loyal to their commanders and are prepared to make sacrifices for them. Lucilius pretends to be Brutus when he is captured so that Brutus can get away safely, and tells Antony that he will never capture Brutus alive. Titinius risks his life for Cassius, and when he finds Cassius has killed himself, Titinius uses the same sword to end his own life. Both are recognized as noble Romans.

Scene Summary

Act I

Rome. A street.

The stage opens with Flavius, Marullus and a group of commoners milling about. Flavius goes up to a couple of workers and asks them what they are doing. He accuses them of being lazy, and demands to know their trade. The first commoner answers that he is a carpenter. Marullus asks the commoner where his tools are, and why he is wearing his best clothes. He then turns to the second carpenter, demanding to know his trade.

The second commoner answers vaguely that he is a cobbler, and Marullus, not satisfied with the tone of the man's statement, tells him to answer the question directly. The commoner calls himself a "mender of soles", as in the soles of shoes, but this is still too vague for Marullus who is now frustrated. He once again asks what the man's trade is, and the commoner tells Marullus not to be mad, adding that if his soles are bad he can mend them. Marullus is offended by the idea that he needs "mending", and asks the commoner the exact meaning of his statement.

Flavius, seeing that Marullus is getting nowhere, intervenes, clarifying that the commoner is a cobbler. The commoner says he is a cobbler and brags on his skill at mending nice shoes. Flavius wants to know why he is not in his shop, and why there are so many men hanging about the streets. The cobbler jokes that the men are out here to wear down their shoes and give him more business, then answers seriously that they are all waiting to see Caesar in his triumphant return.

Marullus mocks Caesar's "victory", asking the carpenter and the cobbler if they remember cheering for Pompey, the man Caesar has defeated, just as they are cheering for Caesar now. He points out the shallowness of cheering for Pompey's victories, as well as his defeat, and insists that Caesar's victory is worth nothing, as it brings no glory to Rome. Marullus then accuses the commoners of being disloyal and tells them to go home and pray.

The commoners leave, and Flavius tells Marullus to go to the Capital and take down and decorations that have been placed on Caesar's statues. Marullus questions whether that is okay, and Flavius assures him it is. Flavius also tells Marullus to drive the commoners indoors wherever he sees them. They want to try and make sure Caesar does not become too popular, and thus too powerful.

The same. A public place.

Caesar, Antony (dressed for the ceremonial run), Calphurnia (Caesar's wife), Portia (Brutus' wife), Pecius, Cicero, Brutus, Cassius, and Casca enter the scene. A sizeable crowd follows them, and along with the crowd comes a Soothsayer, a prophet. Music is playing, and everyone is talking.

Casca quiets the crowd so that Caesar can speak. Caesar calls on his wife, and tells Antony to make sure and touch her during his run. He says that the elders believe a touch from the ceremonial runner will cure barrenness in women. Antony agrees, and states that if Caesar says so, it must be true.

The Soothsayer calls out Caesar's name in the crowd. Caesar hears him and allows him to speak. The Soothsayers tells Caesar to "beware the ides of March" (March 15th). Caesar dismisses the warning and tells everyone to continue on. Everyone exits except for Brutus and Cassius.

Cassius asks Brutus if he is planning on watching the run, and Brutus says no. Cassius then expresses concern for Brutus, saying that, as his friend, he has noticed a change in his temper. Brutus tells him that he has had a lot on his mind, and not to take his behavior as a sign of unfriendliness. Cassius admits he misunderstood Brutus' actions, and also hints that he might know what is troubling Brutus.

Offstage, there is a trumpet and a shout. Brutus hears the trumpet and fears that Caesar has been crowned king. Cassius picks up on this, and asks Brutus if he doesn't want Caesar to be king. Brutus says he loves Caesar, but that he doesn't believe Caesar should be king. Cassius agrees and goes on a tirade about how Caesar is just an ordinary man. He remembers one time they were swimming in the river, and Cassius had to save Caesar because he was weak. He remembers another time where Caesar had a fever in Spain and had a shaking fit. He laments that he should not have to worship someone as ordinary as he is.

Offstage, there is another trumpet sound and more shouts. Brutus again worries that Caesar is having more honors heaped on him. Cassius remarks that Caesar's status is unfair, and wonders why the name "Caesar" is any better than "Brutus" or "Cassius". He admits that in Rome, there is only room for one man, but thinks that could change. Brutus tells Cassius that he gets where he is going with the conversation and says he will think over what Cassius said.

Caesar enters with his train. Caesar looks angry, and Calphurnia looks pale. Cassius tells Brutus to pull on Casca's cloak as he will know what happened.

Caesar calls for Antonius and talks so no one else can hear. He complains that he does not want Cassius close to him anymore, and Antonius tells Caesar that Cassius should not be feared. Caesar arrogantly replies that he does not fear anyone, but also says that Cassius is too observant and unsatisfied with his station. He tells Antonius to come over to his right side, because his left ear is deaf, and tell him his thoughts. Caesar and his group exits except for Casca.

Casca wants to know why Brutus pulled his cloak, and Brutus asks to know what happened. Casca tells them that the shouts occurred each time Caesar was offered a crown by Antony. Caesar refused the crown each time, even though Casca noticed he wanted to keep it badly. After the third refusal, the crowd shouted, and Caesar fainted.

Brutus comments that Caesar must have the "falling sickness" (epilepsy). When Caesar came to he apologized for his behavior, and Cicero spoke something in Greek. Casca did not understand what was said, but knows that Flavius and Marullus were punished for pulling decorations off the statues.

Casca exits after agreeing to have dinner with Cassius later that evening, leaving Brutus and Cassius on the stage. Brutus tells Cassius they will talk tomorrow and exits, as well. Cassius remarks to himself that Brutus is noble, but that he might be swayed. Cassius plans on forging several letters from "commoners" denouncing Caesar and worshipping Brutus instead, and to leave the letters on Brutus' doorstep.

Act I, Scene III

The same. A street. Thunder and lightning.

Casca, carrying a drawn sword, and Cicero enter the stage from opposite sides. They meet in the street, and Cicero greets Casca, asking why is out of breath and staring strangely. Casca remarks that the raging storm must be a sign from heaven. He has seen strange things happen, such as a slave with his hand on fire yet not in pain, a lion in front of the Capitol, women claiming to have seen burning men walking the streets, and an owl in the marketplace during daylight. Casca believes these things to be more than coincidence. Cicero agrees that it is strange, but also says that men will see what they want to in the signs. He then changes the subject, wanting to know if Caesar will be in the Capitol the next day. Casca says he will be, and Cicero exits.

Cassius enters, asking who is there. Casca replies "a Roman", and Cassius recognizes his voice from the reply. Cassius tells Casca that it is a pleasing night "to honest men", and reveals that he has been walking around as if oblivious to the storm, with his shirt unbuttoned. Casca wonders why he would tempt heaven, as the gods are obviously sending a warning along with the thunder and lightning. Cassius tells Casca that he has lost his wits if he cannot see what the signs mean, and states that he can think of one man who has a lot in common with the strange occurrences during the storm. Casca realizes he is talking about Caesar and complains that Caesar is going to be crowned King the next day by the Senate.

Cassius is angered by this news and reveals that he has a dagger he plans to use on himself to commit suicide if Caesar is crowned King. He would rather be dead than be submissive to a tyrant. Casca agrees, and Cassius goes on to rant that Rome is trash if they let a weak man such as Caesar rule. Cassius wants to know if Casca agrees with what he is saying, and Casca does. Not only that, but he promises to support Cassius as far as he is willing to go. The two shake hands, and Cassius reveals that he is on his way to a meeting. Because of the storm, the streets are empty, so it is the ideal time to talk unheard.

Cinna enters the stage. Casca tells Cassius to stop talking because he hears someone approaching. Cassius recognizes Cinna's walk and greets him. Cinna is a fellow conspirator against Caesar and is glad Casca is on their side. Cinna says he was out looking for Cassius, and that the others in the group are waiting for them to return. He also reveals that many of the men have seen strange sights. Cinna believes that if Brutus joins them, they will be successful.

Cassius has a plan to get Brutus' support. He gives Cinna three letters and tells him to place one under Brutus' chair, one inside his window, and the last on the statue of his ancestors. After Cinna is done doing this, he should return to Pompey's house, where the rest of the group is meeting.

Cinna leaves to complete the errand, leaving Cassius and Casca alone again. Cassius is sure that Brutus is almost won over to their cause and hopes the letters will be the final push. Casca admits that the people love Brutus and that his help might be just what they need to succeed. Cassius tells Casca to hurry, they are going to go to Brutus' house and gain his support before sunrise.

Act II

Rome. Brutus' orchard.

Brutus is walking out in his garden, unable to sleep. He calls for Lucius, his servant, to wake up. When Lucius asks him what he needs, he orders a candle to be lit in his chambers and for Lucius to call him when that is done. Lucius leaves, and Brutus muses to himself. He says that Caesar must be killed, even though Brutus himself holds no personal grudge against him. He fears that Caesar's ambition combined with his new-found power as King will corrupt him and turn him into a tyrant. Brutus compares Caesar to a serpent's egg that must be destroyed before it hatches.

Lucius enters to tell Brutus that the candle is lit. He also hands Brutus a letter that he found on his window, still sealed. Brutus takes the letter and tells Lucius that he can go back to sleep as it is not yet dawn. Before Lucius leaves, Brutus asks him if it is the fifteenth of March. Lucius doesn't know and goes to consult a calendar. When Lucius leaves the garden, Brutus opens the letter and begins to read. He puzzles over the letter, trying to figure out its meaning. He comes to the conclusion that the letter is a call to action, thereby reinforcing his previous idea that Caesar must be killed.

Lucius enters the garden again, bringing the news that it is the fifteenth of March. There is a knock at the gate, and Lucius goes to see who it is. When he comes back, he tells Brutus that Cassius has come to see him, along with several other men. When Brutus asks the identities of the others, Lucius admits that they were hiding their faces with their hats and robes and that he could not discern their identities. Brutus tells Lucius to let them in. When Lucius goes to retrieve the visitors, Brutus remarks to himself that they must be the group who is conspiring to kill Caesar.

Cassius enters the orchard, along with the other conspirators including Casca, Decius, Cinna, Metellus and Trebonius. Cassius greets Brutus, hoping that they aren't intruding at such an early hour. Brutus admits that he has been awake all night and asks who Cassius' companions are. Cassius tells Brutus that they are all men who know him well, and admire him. He then introduces them one by one, and Brutus welcomes them all. Cassius asks Brutus for a private word, and they move off to the side, talking softly. Meanwhile, Decius, Casca and Cinna argue about which direction the sun is going to rise in.

Brutus and Cassius return to the group, and Brutus shakes all the men's hands in fellowship. Cassius suggests swearing an oath along with the handshake, but Brutus tells them that only weak men and cowards swear oaths because they are the only ones who would break them. He suggests the group be bound instead by trust and the importance of their mission.

Cassius agrees and turns the talk to planning. He suggests adding Cicero to their group. Casca, Cinna and Metellus all think that he would be a good addition, but Brutus points out that Cicero wouldn't follow the plans of other men. Cassius takes this point and agrees that he wouldn't be suitable. He then suggests also killing Antony, Caesar's right hand man, because his connections might make him a fearful enemy once Caesar is dead. Brutus once again refutes Cassius' point, saying that killing Antony, as well as Caesar, would be too bloody and send the wrong message. He compares Antony to the arm of Caesar, and believes that once Caesar himself is dead Antony will be useless. Cassius is still afraid of Antony, but Brutus insists that he is incapable of hurting anyone but himself in his grief following Caesar's death.

A clock strikes, and the men count three. Cassius says it is time to leave, and wonders if Caesar will even come to the Capitol that day as he has become superstitious of late and many strange things occurred that night. Decius chimes in, assuring the group that he will be able to convince Caesar to come. Cassius says they should all go to the Capitol, and they should be there no later than eight o'clock. Metellus brings up the idea of recruiting Ligarius, and Brutus tells Metellus to send Ligarius to him in the orchard. Cassius and Brutus remind the group to act normal as they go about town, and Brutus says they must be actors putting on a cheerful face. Everyone exits the orchard except for Brutus.

When the men are gone, Portia enters. Brutus asks her why she is up, and the cold morning air is bad for her health. Portia tells Brutus that he has been in a foul mood since the night before and wants to know what is troubling him. Brutus says he is sick, but Portia doesn't buy it, pointing out that if he were indeed sick he would not be out in the cold air so early in the morning. She guesses, correctly, that what is troubling Brutus is in his mind and not his body.

Portia then kneels down and begs to know what is troubling her husband. Brutus tells her not to kneel, and Portia gets up. She tells him that, as his wife she needs to know everything, including his secrets. If he is going to keep her on the outskirts of his business, then she might as well be his whore instead of his wife. When Brutus still won't tell her, she insists that even though she is a woman she is strong, and promises to keep his council to herself. Just then, there is a knock at the gate. Brutus tells Portia to go inside, and promises to tell her what is going on once he has taken care of his visitor. Portia leaves, satisfied.

Ligarius enters the orchard. He is wearing a cloth around his head, signifying that he is sick. Brutus laments that he is unwell, because he had an honorable proposition if only Ligarius was feeling better. Ligarius tells Brutus that if it is truly honorable, then he would be well. When Brutus assures him that it is, Ligarius takes the cloth off his head and asks Brutus what it is. Brutus doesn't tell him right away, instead saying that he will explain while they walk. Ligarius agrees to go and follows Brutus out of the orchard. As they exit the stage, thunder is heard.

The same. A hall in Caesar's palace. Thunder and lightning.

Caesar enters the room in his dressing gown. He has been kept awake by his wife Calphurnia's nightmares. She cried out in her sleep three times that Caesar was murdered. Caesar hears a noise and asks who is there. A servant steps forth, and Caesar orders him to go to the priests and have a sacrifice given. Once this is done, he wants the servant to bring him back news of the result. The servant exits.

Calphurnia enters and asks Caesar what he is doing, saying that he should not leave the house today. Caesar says he is planning on going out, and Calphurnia, normally not superstitious, reminds Caesar of all the strange things that have happened during the night. A lioness gave birth in the streets, graves opened and ghosts began walking, and the heaven is in chaos. Caesar dismisses her concerns, saying that he cannot avoid the will of the God's, and that the signs surely applied to everyone, not just him. Calphurnia insists that omens do not appear for lesser men, but only for princes. Caesar replies that brave men don't fear death, as it is inevitable.

After he says this, a servant enters with bad news. The priests dissected an animal and found no heart. The servant urges Caesar to stay home that day. Caesar is still being stubborn and insists that the heartless animal is a sign saying that if Caesar stays him he will be a heartless coward. Calphurnia gets on her knees and begs Caesar to stay, for her. She suggests sending Antony to the Senate in Caesar's place with the news that Caesar is sick. Caesar finally gives in and promises to stay, but does not want Antony to tell the Senate that he is sick.

Decius enters to take Caesar to the Senate. When Caesar gives the news that he is choosing to stay home, Calphurnia chimes in that he is sick. Caesar is annoyed and asks her why he should lie, as he is not afraid of some grey-haired old men. Decius wants to know the real reason Caesar is staying home, so he won't be laughed at when he goes to the Senate without Caesar. Caesar tells Decius to give the Senate the message that he simply does not wish to appear today, but tells Decius personally that Calphurnia wishes him to stay.

He reveals that Calphurnia had a nightmare in which Caesar's statue was spouting blood, and Romans were bathing in it. She took this as a sign of Caesar's death, but Decius gives another interpretation. He tells Caesar that he is giving Romans sustaining blood, and they are grateful for it. He also tells Caesar that the Senate is planning on giving him a crown and that if he does not show up they will think he is a coward. If they think he is a coward, they might change their minds. Caesar decides to ignore Calphurnia's warnings and go with Decius.

Publius, Brutus, Ligarius, Metellus, Casca, Trebonius and Cinna enter. Caesar greets them and asks for the time. Brutus tells him that is nine o'clock. Antony enters, and Caesar asks that room be prepared for his new guests. He treats them warmly and offers them wine and company. In an aside, Brutus reveals that his heart is aching. They all exit.

Act II, Scene III

The same. A street near the Capitol.

Artemidorus enters the stage, reading a letter. In the letter, he warns Caesar about Brutus, Cassius, and the other conspirators. He plans on waiting until Caesar is walking by and then giving him the letter. He hopes that if Caesar reads the letter in time, that he might live. He exits.

The same. Another part of the same street, before the house of Brutus.

Portia and Lucius enter. Portia tells Lucius to run to the Senate, and Lucius asks her what he should do there. Portia tells him to hurry and leave and says to herself that she has a man's mind but a woman's might, and laments that it is difficult to keep a secret. Lucius again asks for a task to complete while he is there, and Portia asks him to check on Brutus' health as well as taking note of who is around Caesar. She stops, saying she hears a noise. Lucius does not hear anything, but she says it was a rustling coming from the direction of the Capitol.

The Soothsayer enters. Portia greets him, asking him several questions. The Soothsayer tells her it is nine o'clock and that Caesar is not yet at the Capitol. The Soothsayer plans on catching Caesar before he gets there to try and make him listen to his warning. Portia is curious and asks if any harm is going to befall Caesar. The Soothsayer doesn't know for sure, but knows that Caesar is in great danger. He plans on getting ahead of the crowds that are following Caesar in order to talk to him, and leaves.

Portia tells Lucius to hurry to the Senate, and they part going their separate ways.

Act III

In the streets before the Capitol, a crowd is gathering. Artemidorus and the Soothsayer are in the forefront. Trumpets are heard, and Caesar enters, followed by his conspirators as well as others.

Caesar reminds the Soothsayer that it is March fifteenth, and the Soothsayer replies that the day is not over, meaning something bad could still happen. Next, Artemidorus tries to get Caesar to read his letter of warning, disguised as a petition. He tells Caesar that it is of great importance to him personally, and Caesar dismisses him by saying that issues dealing with him directly should be dealt with last. Cassius tells him to give the petition at the Capitol, and not out in the street.

Caesar enters the Capitol, everyone still following. All the Senators rise when Caesar enters. Popilius Lena tells Cassius good luck in his endeavor, and Cassius begins panicking, believing them to be discovered. Popilius talks to Caesar normally, however, and Brutus tells Cassius to calm down. Trebonius exits, taking Antony with him by means of some distraction. Caesar and the Senators take their seats, as Decius, Brutus and Cinna discuss Metellus' suit. They remind each other to support Metellus.

Caesar says that he is ready for session to begin, and Metellus kneels in front of him. Before he can finish his petition, Caesar interrupts him, telling him that flattery will get him nowhere. He already knows what Metellus is going to ask for, his brother to be allowed back from banishment, and Caesar tells Metellus that, as he was banished legally, he will not be allowed back. After Caesar gives his refusal, Brutus gets on his knees and seconds Metellus' petition. Caesar is greatly surprised at this, and even more surprised when the rest of the conspirators, one by one, get on their knees and beg for Metellus' brother's release.

Caesar will not by swayed and compares himself to the northern star in the sky, the one constant among thousands. The conspirators stab Caesar, Brutus last. When Caesar realizes that even Brutus betrayed him, he utters his famous last words "Et tu, Brute? Then fall, Caesar". After saying this, Caesar dies. Brutus laments Caesar's death, saying that his ambition killed him. Publius is frightened, but Brutus reassures him that they won't harm anyone else, and urges him to leave in case the public reacts badly to Caesar's death.

Trebonius enters, with word about the condition outside. He reveals that Antony went to his house stunned and in grief, and that the streets are in chaos. Brutus tells the group that death is inevitable for everyone and comes up with a plan to smear their swords with Caesar's blood and go into the streets shouting "liberty" and "freedom". Cassius agrees with Brutus' plan, noting that, in reenactments, it will be a famous scene. The group then bathes their hands and swords in Caesar's blood.

When they are about to go out into the streets, a servant of Antony's appears. He kneels and tells Brutus that Antony wants to speak with them. He wants proof that Caesar's death was just, but also wants to be guaranteed his safety. Brutus tells the servant that if Antony comes he will leave unharmed. The servant leaves, and Brutus believes that Antony will join them once he has heard their reasons. Cassius is less hopeful, and has a hunch that, instead of welcoming Antony, they should fear him.

Antony arrives, and tells the conspirators that if they are planning to kill him they should do it now, for he is ready to die beside Caesar if that is his fate. Brutus assures Antony that they won't kill him, and tells Antony that they were forced to kill Caesar for the good of Rome. Brutus himself loved Caesar, and pitied him, but action had to be taken. He promises Antony that he will explain the rest of his reasoning later, but tells him to be patient until they have successfully calmed the crowds outside. Antony says he trusts their reasons and shakes all the conspirator's hands, still covered in blood.

Cassius questions Antony's loyalty, but Antony says he will be loyal to them if they have proof that Caesar was dangerous to Rome. Brutus assures Antony that they have proof, and Antony also asks to be able to speak at the marketplace for Caesar's funeral. Brutus agrees to this, but Cassius pulls him aside. He is extremely nervous about allowing Antony to speak as they don't know what affect he might have on the crowd. Brutus believes that by allowing Antony to speak, it will show good faith on their part and will only help their cause. Brutus tells Antony that he can speak as long as he speaks after Brutus. Antony agrees and plans on following them after he prepares the body.

Everyone leaves except for Antony, who addresses Caesar's body. He is disgusted that he had to act so polite around Caesar's murderers to gain their trust, and prophecies that a curse will come upon Rome. A servant enters from Octavius Caesar. Antony remembers that Caesar wrote for Octavius to come to Rome, and the servant tells Antony that Octavius is right outside of town. The servant stops mid-sentence after seeing Caesar's body, and Antony says it is okay for him to weep. He also tells the servant to warn Octavius that it might be dangerous for him to come into Rome. He asks the servant to help carry Caesar's body to the marketplace, hear his funeral, and report back to his master afterward. They leave carrying Caesar's body.

Act III, Scene II

Brutus and Cassius enter the Forum followed by a throng of citizens who are demanding a reason for Caesar's death. Brutus tells them that he is planning to speak and tells Cassius to take the other street. One citizen decides to stay and hear Brutus, while another says he will hear Cassius and compare the reasons the two give. Cassius exits with some citizens following him. Brutus ascends to the pulpit.

Brutus begins his speech by urging the citizens to listen to him in full before judging his actions. He tells them that he loved Caesar dearly but that he loved Rome more. He explains that he believed Caesar to be ambitious, and feared that he would make the people of Rome his slaves. He hints to the crowd that any who are against Caesar's death are not true Romans, and assures them that he is willing to die for Rome's sake when it is his time.

Antony enters with Caesar's body, covered. Brutus bids the crowd to let Antony speak, making sure to point out that, as Caesar's friend and not a conspirator, Antony is only speaking because Brutus is allowing it. The citizens become rowdy. They agree with Brutus and say that it is good Caesar the tyrant is dead. The citizens try to carry Brutus off in triumph to his house, and some state that Brutus should be crowned in Caesar's place. Brutus urges the crowd to calm down, and to listen to Antony speak. Brutus exits.

Antony takes the pulpit. He begins by saying that Brutus and the others are honorable men and that he is not speaking to praise Caesar. Directly following this, however, Antony gives several instances where Caesar did not act ambitiously, including the instance where he refused the crown three times. He then reminds the crowd that Brutus and the others believed Caesar to be ambitious and that they are honorable men. Antony pauses, overcome with emotion.

The citizens begin to murmur, saying that Antony is right. When Antony recovers himself he mentions that Caesar had a will but that he shouldn't read the will for fear of angering the Roman citizens. The citizens urge him several times to read it, and Antony reiterates that Brutus and the others are honorable before relenting. Antony comes down off the pulpit and asks the citizens to form a circle around Caesar's body. Antony pulls off the covering and points out the multiple stab wounds. He makes particular note of Brutus' stab wound.

By this time, the crowd is riled up, and calling for the death of Brutus and the others. Antony urges them to stay as he has not read the will. In Caesar's will, he gives each Roman citizen 75 drachmas and leaves all his property to be converted into public parks. The citizens are enraged, and go off in a mob to find the traitors and kill them. Antony speaks to himself, awed at his ability to manipulate the crowd so easily.

A servant comes in with news that Octavius is already in Rome and that he is waiting at Caesar's house. He also brings news that Brutus and Cassius have been driven out. Antony says he will go see Octavius, and they exit.

Act III, Scene III

A street. Enter Cinna the poet (not Cinna the conspirator) and citizens. Cinna remarks to himself that he had a dream in which he went to a feast with Caesar and it ended unluckily. Just then, some citizens begin questioning him. They ask him his name, where he is going, where he lives, and if he is married. They also urge him to answer quickly and truthfully.

Cinna replies that he is a bachelor and that he is going to Caesar's funeral. A citizen interrupts to ask if he is going as a friend or an enemy, and Cinna replies a friend. He continues to say that he lives near the Capitol and that his name is Cinna. The citizens immediately seize him as a conspirator, shouting for his death. Cinna insists that he is a poet, but they ignore his protests and drag him off anyway. They then split up into groups to find the other conspirators.

Act IV

At Antony's house, Antony, Octavius and Lepidus sit around a table. They are making conditions on who should die. Octavius points out that, under Antony's conditions, Lepidus' brother will be killed. Lepidus gives his consent to this, pointing out that one of Antony's relatives is also suspect. He will allow his brother to be killed if Antony also gives no mercy to his own relatives. Antony says this is fair and asks Lepidus to go to Caesar's house and find the will. He wants to see if there is any way to get some of his funds to save money. Lepidus leaves, promising to find them later at either Antony's house or the Capitol.

When Lepidus is gone, Antony questions whether or not he is an honorable enough man to help guide Rome in this time of turmoil. Antony likens Lepidus to a donkey only fit for bearing burdens that Antony and Octavius don't want to deal with. Octavius defends Lepidus, saying he is a noble and valiant soldier. Antony responds by saying his horse is a valiant soldier as well, and Lepidus must be trained in the same manner. He urges Octavius not to speak of Lepidus as anything more valuable than property, and then changes the subject to more weighty matters. Antony reveals that Brutus and Cassius are gathering their forces outside of the city and suggests that Octavius accompany him to the council so that they may do the same. Octavius agrees, stating that they are surrounded by many enemies and need all the strength they can get. They exit.

Before Brutus' tent, in the camp near Sardis. A drum is heard. Brutus enters along with Lucilius, his commander, Lucius, and the army. Titinius and Pindarus (Cassius' commanders) meet them.

Brutus asks if Cassius is near, and Lucilius confirms that he is. He also tells Brutus that Pindarus is here to see him with a word from his master, Cassius. Pindarus asks Brutus if Cassius could be allowed to see him, and Brutus consents. Just to be safe, Brutus asks Lucilius, who visited Cassius earlier, how Cassius received him. Lucilius tells Brutus that Cassius was polite and respectful but not as friendly as he used to be. Brutus is afraid that Cassius is displeased with him and does not want to make another enemy. Lucilius also reveals that Cassius' army is quartered in Sardis and that some of them will come with Cassius when he visits Brutus.

Cassius enters with his soldiers. He tells Brutus that he has wronged him, and Brutus wants to know how he has done so. Brutus asks Cassius to call off his soldiers so that they may speak as friends, and Cassius consents. Cassius tells Pindarus to lead his soldiers a little ways off, and Brutus asks Lucilius to do the same with his soldiers. Brutus leaves Lucius and Titinius to guard the tent and make sure no one enters.

Brutus and Cassius enter Brutus' tent. Cassius immediately accuses Brutus of wronging him by punishing one of Cassius' friends who was charged of accepting bribes. Cassius wrote to Brutus, and claims Brutus ignored him. Brutus chides Cassius for writing the letter in the first place, and Cassius accuses Brutus of being too strict at such a tense time. Brutus tells Cassius that he is greedy and has been known to give away offices to less than honorable men for money. Cassius, in turn, is outraged at this accusation and tells Brutus that only his respect for him as a friend is keeping him alive after such a statement.

Brutus goes on to say that Cassius' crimes have not been punished, and Cassius is once again indignant. Brutus points out that they killed Caesar for justice and for fear of how corrupted he would become if allowed to rule unheeded. He does not want that same corruption to run rampant in the system, or Caesar's death would have been for nothing. Cassius warns Brutus not to go any farther as he is an older soldier and better at giving orders. They argue about this for a little while before Brutus tells Cassius that he is not afraid of him or his fury. While Cassius' temper might frighten other people, Brutus feels that he is in the right and thus has no shame. He asks Cassius to prove that he is the better soldier.

Cassius corrects Brutus, saying that he never called himself the better soldier, but the older one. Brutus does not care, and Cassius lashes out at him, stating that even Caesar would not have provoked him so. Brutus believes Cassius would not have provoked Caesar for fear of his life. Cassius is getting steadily angrier and warns Brutus that if things go on like this he will do something he will regret.

Brutus gets to the heart of the matter. Apparently Brutus asked Cassius for gold to pay his soldiers. He did not want to ask the poor peasants for money, and turned to Cassius instead. Brutus' request was refused, and Brutus is angry at Cassius for being so greedy when so much is at stake. Cassius tells Brutus that he did not refuse his request and that the messenger must have given him the wrong message. Cassius then accuses Brutus of not loving him, as he was so quick to exaggerate Cassius' faults. Brutus is still not satisfied with Cassius' response and tells Cassius that he does not like his faults.

At this, Cassius calls on Antony and Octavius to hurry and end his life as he has lost his last friend. Cassius takes out his dagger and bares his chest, telling Brutus to carve out his heart so he can die a true Roman. Calming down, Brutus tells Cassius to put the dagger away and apologizes because he was in a bad mood. Cassius thinks Brutus is making fun of him, but Brutus assures him that he is not angry anymore.

They shake hands, and Cassius is grateful that Brutus can put up with his foul temper.

Offstage, a poet speaks to the guards. He wants to see the generals and insists that they shouldn't be left alone. Lucilius tells the poet he is not allowed inside the tent, but the poet enters, saying they would have to kill him before he stopped. The poet steps inside, followed by Lucilius, Titinius and Lucius. He then addresses Brutus and Cassius, telling them to quit arguing and to remain friends. Already reconciled, Brutus and Cassius mock the poet's rhymes before sending him back out.

Once the poet is gone, Brutus tells Lucilius and Titinius to have the men lodge where they are tonight, and Cassius tells them to bring Messala back after they are done with their errand. Lucilius and Titinius exit, and Brutus asks Lucius to bring him some wine. When Lucius leaves, Cassius remarks that he didn't know Brutus could even get that angry at anybody. Brutus says he was only taking out his grief over Portia's death. Surprised,

Cassius asks how she died. Brutus tells him that he received a letter detailing the strange manner of her death. Worrying about Brutus, and fearing that Antony and Octavius have grown too powerful, Portia gave into despair and committed suicide by "swallowing fire". Cassius is sorrowful, and Lucius reenters the tent with wine.

Brutus doesn't want to talk anymore, but would rather drink to drown his sorrows. In response, Cassius fills their glasses to the brim. Brutus calls for Titinius and Lucius goes to fetch Titinius, waiting outside the door with Messala in tow. Brutus welcomes Messala and asks to talk strategy. He wants to know if Messala has received any new intelligence, as Brutus has knowledge that Antony and Octavius are moving their growing army towards Philippi. Messala has heard the same, but also that Antony and Octavius have killed a hundred senators for treason against the Capitol. Brutus heard only seventy were killed, but that Cicero was among them. Cassius is shocked at this.

Messala asks Brutus if he has heard any news of Portia. Brutus says he hasn't, and Messala thinks that is strange. When Brutus pushes, however, Messala tells him that Portia has died. Brutus puts on a strong face, saying that everyone must die and that he can endure his pain. Messala is in admiration of Brutus' control, and Cassius can't believe how calm Brutus is. Brutus changes the subject back to strategy, asking Cassius' opinion of marching toward Philippi. Cassius doesn't think marching toward the enemy is a good idea, as they should save their strength for defense and let the enemy wear their army out before they get to the battlefield. Brutus thinks that is a good point, but disagrees with Cassius, arguing that Antony and Octavius' army grows stronger every day, while Brutus and Cassius' army is already at their full strength. He believes they should take advantage of this while they can, and launch a preemptive attack. Cassius relents, and they agree to sleep a short while before leaving at dawn for the battlefield.

Cassius leaves, bidding Brutus goodnight, and Lucius fetches Brutus his nightgown. Brutus asks Lucius to call Claudius, and Varro and Claudius enter. Brutus wants them to stay in the tent tonight as he might have messages to run to Cassius in the morning. He lets them lay down, even though they say they can guard him standing. Brutus then asks Lucius to play his instrument, and music starts up. Soon, however, even Lucius is nodding, and Brutus takes the instrument from him before he falls in his sleep and breaks it. Still not able to sleep, Brutus begins reading to calm his mind.

Caesar's ghost enters the tent, and Brutus is confused. He wants to know who or what the ghost is, and Caesar tells Brutus that he will see him again at Philippi. Caesar's ghost vanishes, and Brutus wakes up Lucius, Varro and Claudius, asking them if they saw or heard anything. All of them were asleep and didn't hear anything. Brutus asks Varro and Claudius to go to Cassius and tell him to begin moving soldiers out. Brutus' army will follow afterward. Everyone exits.

Act V

On the plains of Philippi, Octavius, Antony, and their army enter. Octavius makes note of the fact that Brutus and Cassius have come down from the hills, which is what they hoped would happen. Antony is still wary and tells Octavius that they are just trying to appear brave, but know that they have the disadvantage. A messenger enters, alerting the generals of the opposing army's advancement. Antony tells Octavius to lead his army left, but Octavius refuses, saying he will go to the right and Antony to the left. Antony asks Octavius why he should disagree, but Octavius insists that he take the right. They begin marching towards the field of battle.

Drums are heard, and Brutus, Cassius and their army, including Lucilius, Titinius and Messala enter. Brutus notices that Octavius and Antony have stopped, and Cassius says they should talk before the battle begins. On the other side, Octavius asks Antony if they should prepare to attack, but Antony tells him to wait, as it is customary for generals to exchange words before the battle.

Meeting in the middle of the field, the conversation quickly degenerates into insults and threats. Antony is angry at Caesar's death, and accuses Brutus and Cassius of being traitors. Cassius, in turn, accuses Antony of using honey-sweet words to manipulate the population. Octavius swears he will avenge the death of Caesar, and Brutus promises to kill Octavius with the same sword that killed Caesar. The two parties leave on bad terms, and Octavius, Antony and their army exit after telling Brutus and Cassius to meet them in the field.

When the opposing army is gone, Brutus takes Lucilius aside for a private word. While they are talking, Cassius calls for Messala. He reveals to Messala that it is his birthday and that he has seen bad omens. At the beginning of the march, two eagles sat on the banners, but now they have been replaced with ravens and other scavenger birds. Messala tells Cassius not to pay attention to these signs, and to have hope. Brutus and Lucilius return, and Cassius notes to Brutus that if the day goes badly they will never see each other again. They bid farewell to each other and exit.

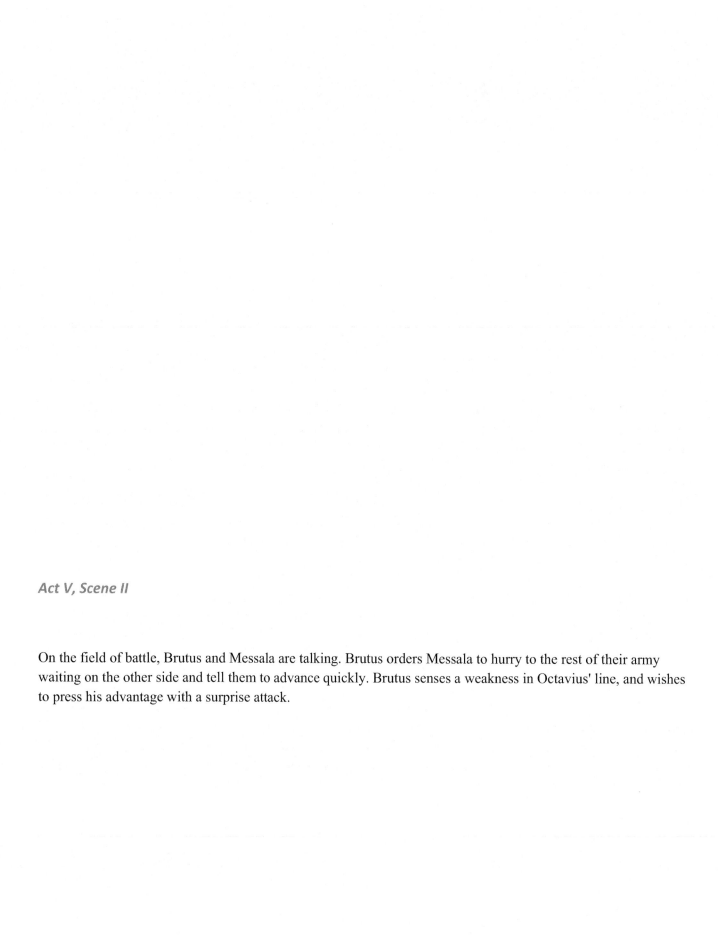

Act V, Scene II

On the field of battle, Brutus and Messala are talking. Brutus orders Messala to hurry to the rest of their army waiting on the other side and tell them to advance quickly. Brutus senses a weakness in Octavius' line, and wishes to press his advantage with a surprise attack.

Another part of the field. Drums are heard, and Cassius and Titinius enter. Cassius tells Titinius that he cannot believe his own soldiers flee the field of battle. Titinius blames Brutus, seeing that his attack on Octavius was over-eager, and now they are surrounded by Antony's men. Pindarus enters, telling Cassius to get somewhere farther away because Antony has entered his camp. Cassius asks if those are his tents burning, and Pindarus says yes.

Cassius then asks Titinius to go toward the camp and check on the approaching troops to see if they are friends or enemies. Titinius leaves and Pindarus goes up to the top of the hill to see what happens. He tells Cassius that Titinius is being chased down by some unknown men and that they catch up with him, forcing him to dismount. A shout of joy is heard, and Cassius, believing Titinius to be fallen, tells Pindarus to come back down. Cassius gives Pindarus his sword, the same sword that killed Caesar, and tells him to run it through him. Cassius dies, and Pindarus, a free man, runs away, hoping to get as far away from Rome as possible.

Titinius and Messala enter the scene. Titinius is pleased because, although the tides of battle have turned, no side has a distinct advantage yet. Octavius' troops were overcome by Brutus' army, and Cassius' troops were overcome by Antony's army. Suddenly, they notice Cassius lying on the ground, dead. Titinius is sorrowful, and Messala goes to give the unpleasant news to Brutus.

Alone with Cassius, Titinius reveals that the approaching troops were Brutus', and they stopped Titinius to gives him a crown of victory to pass on to Cassius. Titinius places the crown on Cassius' head, and then kills himself with Cassius' sword.

Messala enters with Brutus, young Cato, Strato, Volumnius and Lucilius. Brutus asks where the body is, and Messala directs them to the hill, where Titinius is now slain next to Cassius. Brutus blames Caesar's vengeful ghost for turning their swords against their own men, and claims that Cassius and Titinius were true Romans. However, they cannot hold a service for them in the midst of battle, so it will have to wait. It is still the afternoon, and Brutus goes back to the battlefield to reengage the enemy.

There is fighting, and the soldiers of both armies are on the field. Brutus, young Cato, Lucilius and others enter. Brutus encourages his men to stay strong, and he and young Cato run out into the midst of battle.

Lucilius, trying to see what happens, says that young Cato is down and that he died bravely. While he is watching, some soldiers appear. They tell Lucilius to yield or die, and Lucilius, purposefully calling himself Brutus, tells the soldiers to kill him. They take him alive as a prisoner of war and give him to Antony. Antony quickly realizes that he is not the real Brutus, but tells the soldiers to treat him kindly, as he is a worthy man. Antony asks Lucilius where Brutus is, and Lucilius boldly states that he will never find Brutus alive.

Act V, Scene V

Brutus and his few remaining men, Dardanius, Clitus, Strato and Volumnius take a rest. Clitus marks that Statilius is not back and must have been killed. Brutus asks Clitus to sit, and whispers in his ear. After, Clitus tells Brutus that he would rather kill himself. Brutus then goes to Dardanius and whispers to him, as well. Dardanius also refuses Brutus' request. Clitus asks Dardanius what Brutus asked of him, and Dardanius says Brutus asked Dardanius to kill him.

Meanwhile, Brutus is asking Volumnius the same question, and Volumnius also refuses. Brutus tells him that Caesar's ghost has appeared to him twice, once in Sardis and once on the battlefield at Philippi. Because of this, Brutus is certain that his hour has come to die. Volumnius still refuses, and Brutus asks him to just hold the sword while he runs on to it. Clitus yells that they must leave because the enemy is almost on them. Brutus bids his men farewell, stating that even though they lost he will go down in glory.

Drums are heard along with cries of "fly, fly, fly". Brutus tells his men to go on ahead, and Dardanius, Clitus and Volumnius exit. Strato is the only one who stays behind, and Brutus asks him to hold the sword steady so he can have a clean death. Strato shakes his hand and bids Brutus farewell. Brutus runs into the sword and, as he is dying, says that he killed himself with purer intentions than he killed Caesar with, and that Caesar's spirit should be satisfied. Brutus dies.

Octavius, Antony, Messala, Lucilius and the army enter. Octavius, not knowing who Strato is, asks Messala. Messala reveals Strato to be one of Brutus' men and asks where Brutus is. Strato replies that Brutus is now free of all bonds, and Lucilius is glad that he was not taken alive by the enemy. Octavius asks Brutus' men to join him, and they relent. Antony stands over Brutus' body and proclaims him the most noble of Romans. While the other conspirators acted out of envy and greed, only Brutus acted for the good of the people. Octavius agrees that Brutus deserves every respect and vows to give him a ceremonious burial. They express joy in their victory, and depart.

The Life and Times of William Shakespeare

The Times Shakespeare Lived In

The Elizabethan London that William Shakespeare arrived in was much different than it is today. Significantly, the population was much smaller. Today, seven and a half million people live in the area known as Greater London. In Shakespeare's time the population was around 200,000 – this still made it an enormous metropolis for the time period and it was the leading city in Europe.

In the sixteenth century London suffered from an extremely high death rate – more people died in the city than were born. It was only the steady influx of newcomers from other English counties and immigrants from Europe that helped London's population grow. The bubonic plague was still a large factor in death counts in the city – in fact many people fled the urban area when the many epidemics rolled through. Shakespeare himself probably returned at times to Stratford when it was healthier to do so. The life expectancy in London at the time was thirty-five years; this seemingly short life expectancy would be lengthened if one survived childhood – many children did not make it to their fifth birthday.

London was a crowded and dirty place – it is not surprising that disease was rampant. The houses were built close together and the streets were very narrow – in many cases only wide enough for a single cart to navigate. There was no indoor plumbing and it would be another three hundred years before a sanitary way of disposing of sewage was built for the city of London.

Shakespeare was born into a time of religious upheaval. The Catholic Church came under pressure from the second Tudor ruler, Henry VIII, to annual his first marriage to Catherine of Aragon. Upon the death of his brother Arthur and Henry's ascendancy to the heir to the English throne, he had married his brother's widow in 1509. Over the years Catherine had given birth to only one surviving heir – a daughter Mary. Twenty-four years later, Henry asked for a divorce so he could marry the young Anne Boleyn. The Pope refused and in 1534 Henry broke from the Church, establishing the Church of England. The throne went to Henry's son Edward VI in 1547 but upon the boy's death in 1553, his half-sister Mary, daughter of Henry and Catherine, became Queen. She was a devout Catholic, and plunged the country back into a period of dissension and conflict, which included persecution and death for Protestants and the re-establishment of the Roman Catholic Church.

Queen Mary's death changed the religious *status quo* in England once again when Queen Elizabeth I came to the throne in 1558. The Catholic Church was once again banned, and the Church of England resurrected in its stead.

England also faced a turning point in its very political existence during Shakespeare's "lost years", those years before his arrival in London when his little is known about his life. In 1588, after Elizabeth I had condemned her cousin Mary, Queen of Scots, to death for conspiracy Spain decided to attack Britain in retaliation for the Roman Catholic Mary's death. The Catholic powers were increasingly fearful of the Protestant movement and with England's break from the Church of Rome now seemingly the final stroke in their relationship, it looked as though Catholicism itself was under threat. Spain rose of fleet of ships to sail upon England and it was thought to be unbeatable. However several factors led to English victory – strategic mistakes on the Spanish side and poor weather were among them. England emerged triumphant, its confidence strong, and the Church of England firmly entrenched. Queen Elizabeth I, known as "Gloriana" always serves as a backdrop to any story of Shakespeare's life. An interesting development during her reign was the acceleration of literacy in Elizabethan England – by the end of her reign, it stood at 33% (probably for males only) and was one of the highest rates in the world.

Queen Elizabeth's reign ended in 1603, when she died in her sleep at the age of sixty-nine. Her cousin's son, James I of Scotland became England's king. He was devoutly Protestant so there was no change in the official

Church, and indeed by the beginning of the 17th century, few English citizens had ever attended a Catholic mass.

James enthusiastically supported drama and in particular, Shakespeare's company. Over the next thirteen years, before William's death, the playwright's company would perform for the King one hundred and eighty seven times. It was the time of Shakepeare's greatest dramatic output.

Much information on the London theatres of the day has been gleaned from the journal and business papers of Philip Henslowe, who owned the Rose and Fortune theatres. For his papers we can extrapolate what life for actors and playwrights would have been like during Shakespeare's time. We also know something of the Fortune Theatre's building – the contract to build it has survived. These records were used to build the copy of the Globe Theatre that stands on the banks of the Thames River today. Other information has come from existing diaries and letters that survived the time – mostly from visitors to the city who found the whole experience interesting enough to record.

Shakepeare's Family

William Shakespeare, the son of John Shakespeare and Mary, née Arden, was born in the village of Stratford-upon-Avon in the English county of Warwickshire. Stratford is northwest of London, situated somewhat south of England's center. Shakespeare was born quite possibly on 23 Apr in 1564 – his baptism in the family's parish church on April 26 suggests this. Children in that day and age were often baptized on the third day after their birth.

William was John and Mary's third known child – and the first to survive infancy. His two older sisters, Joan and Margaret, both died before he was born. Of the five younger children (Gilbert, a second Joan, Anne, Richard, and Edmund) Anne died at the age of eight but William's other siblings lived into adulthood. Only the second Joan was to reach what we would consider a good old age – she died in 1646 at the age of seventy-seven.

William's background on his paternal side was, like most of the English of his day, humble. Earlier relatives were not gentry in the least but simple tenant farmers who worked in the parish of nearby Arden. The meaning of the name Shakespeare has long been shrouded in mystery – the rarity of the surname indicates that it probably originated with one man several hundred years before William's birth. Evidence shows that the first Shakespeare was born somewhere north of Warwickshire. By 1389 an Adam Shakespeare was a tenant farmer at Baddesley Clinton in Warwickshire – unfortunately early parish records were not compelled to be kept until not long before William's time so it is not known for sure if he was a direct ancestor. In 1596 William's father John applied for a family coat of arms, citing that his grandfather had been granted land in northern Warwickshire for service under Henry VII in the War of the Roses. Historians believe this was probably a valid claim, but no records have come to light that prove it.

William was the grandson of Richard Shakespeare, a tenant farmer at Snitterfield in Arden who was not a wealthy man but did leave a will in which he named John Shakespeare as administrator, which would indicate he was the eldest surviving son. By the time of Richard's death in 1560, John had been living at nearby Stratford-upon-Avon since 1550. Records show that John had his first house in Henley Street in Stratford by 1552 and had acquired the house next door and one in Greenhill Street by 1556. John's trade was that of a glove-maker and he also worked as a wool dealer and an animal skin-cutter. He may have also worked as a butcher - it would seem that he was a man who was not afraid of work and had some ambition to better himself.

Around 1557 John Shakespeare married Mary Arden, the daughter of the owner of the Snitterfield estate where his father Richard Shakespeare farmed. Mary was the youngest of the eight daughters of Robert Arden – apparently Robert had a hand in marrying his daughters off and John must have seemed a likely prospect at the time – certainly on the social scale the Ardens would have been higher than the Shakespeares.

On his mother's side at least, William's roots in the area were deep. Just to the north of the River Avon is the village of Arden, from which Mary's family undoubtedly took their name. Surnames were beginning to be "set" about four hundred years before William's birth; it is probable that that branch of the family had been in the area for at least that long.

William's grandfather Robert Arden was a man of some means, at least locally. He owned several estates, including the one where Richard Shakespeare was a tenant farmer. The Ardens were Roman Catholic – England at the time was seesawing between the old Catholic Church and Protestantism. Although the marriage is not found in a surviving record, it is likely that it took place at Aston Cantlow where Mary's father had been buried in 1556 and the ceremony would have been a Catholic one, as Mary Tudor, who had brought Catholicism back to England as the official church, was on the throne. Not long before William's birth in 1564 Elizabeth I became

Queen of England and the country made the final break with Roman Catholicism, and the local parish church became part of the new Church of England.

Shakespeare's Childhood and Education

William Shakespeare's accepted birth date of April 23, 1564 has long been open to dispute, but the month and year are probably correct. There are two reasons April 23rd is the sentimental favorite: it is St. George's Day in England (George is the country's patron saint) and Shakespeare died on the same date fifty-two years later. Baby William was baptized on the 26th of April in the parish church of Stratford-upon-Avon and as infants in Tudor times were traditionally baptized on the third day following their birth, historians have happily settled on the 23rd as his date of birth.

William was the third of eight known children born to John Shakespeare and Mary (Arden) Shakespeare, and the first to survive infancy. In fact young William's first year was overshadowed by the spectre of the Black Death, now known more prosaically as the bubonic plague. About 10% of the residents of Stratford died that year and the Shakespeares' must have felt relief their young family's survival. The plague was to continue to be a problem for England's citizens during the Elizabethan era. William was to lose his younger sister, eight-year-old Anne, to the disease. Quite possibly his older sister Margaret, a one-year-old baby, died of the Black Death as well, as it swept through the area in 1563. The survival of William, as the first born son, and after the deaths of older sisters Joan and Margaret, no doubt gave him a special place in the Shakespeare family.

William's childhood home, in Henley Street, Stratford, is still standing and is a typical Tudor structure with decorative half timber and small windows. In Shakespeare's time the house would have had a thatched roof. Henley Street led out of town and William apparently spent much time as a boy wandering and playing the countryside near at hand. He undoubtedly spoke the local dialect and though his own speech was probably more refined due to his education - and undoubtedly influenced by his mother, who came from a higher social stratum than the Shakespeares – William retained a good "ear" for dialectic speech which is evident in his plays and apparently retained his Warwickshire accent until his death.

William's life as a youngster was rural. His father was a craftsman and a tradesman – a glover and maker of leather goods – and records show that neighbors included a tailor and a haberdasher. But also nearby was a blacksmith – who's trade in those times would have been mostly horses – and shepherds lived nearby. As William rambled around the countryside he would have come into contact with the rural inhabitants of various occupations and he would have been well versed in the area's flora and fauna. It is very likely that he knew all the local fairy stories and tales of ghosts, witches, and hobgoblins, which England's rural denizens of the era were particularly fond of these stories. William's later writings show that he was well acquainted with the terms and practices of the rural pursuits of hunting and fishing – like most of his male contemporaries of the time, the young William probably spent many a happy hour engaged in these activities.

As the son of an alderman, William was entitled to a free education. His father John had become an alderman when William was just a baby – John was appointed to replace another alderman who got himself into trouble with the town council. By 1568 he was elected as an alderman and three years later was chief alderman and deputy to the local bailiff (the town's top magistrate). John was involved in local politics for many years, and although his fortunes and position faltered in later years, his son William was guaranteed the best education Stratford could offer.

William's learning took place at King's New School – which is still operating as a boy's school today. The school was originally granted a charter in 1553 by the learned young King Edward VI – a number of schools were erected in his name. It is thought the school was the last of the King Edward Schools as the adolescent Edward died only nine days after its charter was granted. It was familiarly known as the King's New School, and sometimes shortened even more to New School. Today it is known as King Edward VI School (or K.E.S.) and while no records exist from Shakespeare's time, it is generally accepted that William was a pupil and would have begun his education there around 1570 about the time he turned six years old.

The average school day for the middle class boys of Stratford was not an easy one. Students arrived early in the morning, not long after dawn, and remained in school until 5 PM. Breaks were given for meals. The boys also attended school on Saturdays. Church attendance was part of the school day, and much time was given over to the learning of the classical languages and translating classical texts. The Roman poet Ovid made a strong impression on young William. Classical mythology is evident in William's later works and no doubt their influence can be traced back to those formative days in Stratford's New School.

William probably left school around the age of fifteen. What he did then has not been documented but in the normal course of things, he would have worked for his father, at least for a time. He may have also been a school master – his facility with words and his sharp intellect would have made him a good candidate – but perhaps it was simply not his avocation and as time would prove, writing was. Within a few years, though, William was married. Marriage at eighteen in those days was relatively rare – physical maturation coming later to the young of that era compared to today. William, however, had been courting an older woman, and as nature took its course, Anne Hathaway became pregnant. Pregnant brides were common among the rural population – in fact many believed that fertility should be proven before heading for the altar! William Shakespeare and Anne Hathaway were married by license and as William was under twenty-one, he had to obtain his father's consent to marry. The actual parish where their wedding ceremony took place is not known, though it may have been in Shottery, Anne's home parish.

Shakepeare's Adulthood

By the time William Shakespeare was twenty-one years old, he had become the father of three children. His wife Anne gave birth to daughter Susanna in May 1583 and to twins Judith and Hamnet early in 1785. William does appear in an existing legal record for Stratford concerning property owned by his parents in 1786. Unfortunately very little else is on record for the years before he appears in London.

William most likely remained in Stratford for the first few years of his marriage and his knowledge of leather indicates that he probably worked with his glove-making father after he left school. The story that he had been a school master or tutor has long been conjectured. A story of William teaching in a more the Catholic-friendly county of Lancashire has been bandied about. None of the stories have any real evidence to back them up, however.

William and Anne lived in the house on Henley Street with his parents. It is hard to conceive that he would have deserted his wife and children when the latter were so young – William came from a comfortable solidly middle class family and he would have likely been taught to fulfill his responsibilities. Shakespeare may have spent his working career in London, and hints of philandering came forth, but he always remained faithful to Stratford and returned often and in middle age, he returned for good. How happy or unhappy he and Anne were together is simply not known. The fact that no children were born to Anne after the twins arrived may speak volumes – but it may also simply be that the birth of twins rendered her unable to have more children. That William did send home much of his acquired wealth in London does at least indicate that he had not entirely deserted his family responsibilities – but whether it was done out of love or duty, we do not have any way of knowing. The years between 1585 and 1592 are considered Shakespeare's "lost years". Simply put, there is no hard evidence of what William was doing during those years.

We also know little about William's wife Anne – she was one of seven children of Richard Hathaway, a yeoman farmer. She was left a small sum of money in his will when he died the year before her marriage and she was to come into this inheritance upon her marriage. The house she grew up in, known as Anne Hathaway's Cottage, is now open to the public, but is more than a mere cottage, having twelve rooms. It is about a mile from the center of Stratford. Anne's gravestone is still in existence as well, and from it her approximate date of birth is calculated – it records that she died in 1623, aged sixty-seven. No verified portraits of her exist and there is no known written description of what she looked like. Some Shakespearean experts believe that Sonnet 145 was written for Anne – the sonnet only really makes sense when the reader understands the wordplay with "hate" and "away" – close enough to mimic her surname, Hathaway.

What were William's influences before he arrived in London to make his way in the world of drama? Certainly he had enjoyed a classical education as a lad and some historians that theorized that he was somehow exposed to more in his late teens and twenties – even if only as a schoolmaster. As for the world of the stage, despite Shakespeare living in a somewhat isolated and rural area, it was quite common for bands of actors to be traveling the countryside plying their trade. These plague haunted years drove many people out of London and into the healthier countryside and actors had to make a living too. They were not above staging performances wherever they could gather enough people to pay the entrance fee. Actors were usually required to have a patron and many wore a badge that identified him as such – this kept the local authorities from looking upon actors as a liability to their parishes. The companies were often sponsored by men of means and even by the nobility. The first acting company created in the reign of Queen Elizabeth I (who came to the throne in 1558) was Lord Leicester's Men in 1574 – the Earls of Sussex and Oxford also had companies by 1582. There was rivalry between the companies and apparently, the Lord Mayor of London disliked the acting groups intensely. Unfortunately, few records for the acting companies have survived.

At least one acting company, The Queen's Men, put in more than one appearance at Stratford in 1589 – and if William was still living there, he very well could have attended their performances. Again, precisely why Shakespeare went to London is not known – but he may have simply been seduced by the theatre life and combined with his love of words it would have seemed the perfect home for him. Again, conjecture comes into deciding Shakespeare's life (one theory has it that William had clung to the old Catholic ways and went to northern England where there was more toleration) but his reasons for going to London remain a mystery. Fortunately for the literary world, he *was* drawn to the theatre and left a stunning literary legacy.

What did William do once he reached London? Again, we don't know for sure, as there are few employment records that have survived from centuries past. Shakespeare did appear in the London in the late 1580's and if he was immediately attracted to the theatre, he would have headed to Southwark, on the south side of the Thames, where many of the restrictions of the city of London did not apply. The entertainment industry of its day was free to do as they wanted there. A tradition has survived down through the centuries that William first got a job holding horses outside the theatre and then moved up to be a prompter's assistant. It is known that within a few years William was "becoming Shakespeare" and was writing.

With so many blanks to fill in his life and so very little solid evidence of Shakespeare's very existence at this point, how is it known that he was writing by 1592? It is thanks to one Robert Greene, another London writer. Greene published an attack on William, accusing him of plagiarism and calling him an "upstart crow". Greene parodied some lines from the history play *Henry VI Part III* and intimated that Shakespeare was stealing from his competition. Greene died soon after this, but the publisher of the attack apologized in print – which indicates that William, still a young man at twenty-eight, had enough of a reputation or at least enough gall, to demand a retraction.

If *Henry VI Part III* had already been written by 1592, there is a good chance that Parts I and II had already been penned as well. This accomplishment would have been remarkable for such a young man, and one who had not attended university as well. His lack of higher education seemed to be an issue with some of his contemporary writers – snobbism not being exclusive to the modern world. Fellow writers, who looked at Shakespeare critically and no doubt enviously, included Christopher Marlowe and Thomas Nashe.

Henry VI Part III was not William's first play. *The Two Gentlemen of Verona* was written sometime between 1588 and 1590. Although it is difficult to determine exactly when many of his early plays were written, it is thought that *A Comedy of Errors* might have been his first comedic play and could have been written as early as 1591. In 1594, Shakespeare created Titus Andronicus, his first attempt at tragedy.

There is nothing in the scant surviving records to suggest that William worked for a theatrical company during his early years in London. It is very likely he worked as a freelance writer, as many of contemporaries of the time did. Looking again at his private life, it is possible that during his early years he was returning home to Stratford at regular intervals.

It is thought that during his early years, he worked with other writers to produce collaborative works. *Sir Thomas More*, a historical play about the martyred Thomas More who was executed by Henry VIII, was co-written with Anthony Munday and Henry Chettle, the latter being the very publisher who retracted Robert Greene's accusation of plagiarism in 1592. Experts believe this was written during Shakespeare's early period.

It is known that it didn't take long for William's work to attract the interest of several different theatrical companies. *Titus Andronicus* was first performed by Sussex's Men. Pembroke's Men also performed several of William's plays and at least two known performance venues are on record – The Inns of Court and the Bankside

Rose playhouse. Some Shakespearean historians believe that William had joined the Queen's Men on tour before he arrived in London – some of his later plays are similar to plays they performed in the mid 1580's.

The theatres of London were not a stable entity in the 1590's. Once again, the pall of the plague hung over the city in the summer of 1592. The Puritans, a Protestant faction that had gained some power in the Elizabethan era, despised what they saw as the licentiousness of theatre life and pressured the city to shut down acting venues in London and Southwark. They blamed the theatres for spreading the Plague. The theatres remained closed for two years.

Whether William remained in London for the duration of the Plague years is unknown, but it is known that he turned to writing poetry. In 1593 the rather racy poem *Venus and Adonis* appeared and was dedicated to Henry Wriothesley, the Earl of Southampton. The Earl was a patron of the arts – he supported several poets and often attended the theatre. Shakespeare may have looked upon him as opportunity knocking; after all, having a patron was easier that freelancing. It has been conjectured that Shakespeare's poems were written to Wriothesley as expressions of love and passion; many have conjectured that Shakespeare had homosexual or bisexual leanings. This could be or it might just be that Shakespeare saw an opportunity and wrote what Wriothesley wanted. Without solid evidence, it is impossible to know.

Shakespeare also dedicated the more serious and tragic poem *The Rape of Lucrece* to Wriothesley in 1594. It was about a Roman married woman who is raped by a Roman prince – she then commits suicide. The Rape of Lucrece was not quite as successful as Venus and Adonis but by now Shakespeare's reputation as a writer was established.

William returned to play writing once the Plague had died down again by the fall of 1594. A new theatrical company was formed by Lord Hunsdon (who was Queen Elizabeth's Lord Chamberlain), and called the Chamberlain's Men. Evidence has survived that indicate that Shakespeare was part of the company. Richard Burbage was also part of Chamberlain's Men – he became the company's star actor and would be the lead in many of the Shakespeare plays that they performed. Many of the actors who belonged to the company also had a financial stake in it.

The Chamberlain's Men did well from the start. They first performed for theatre-owner Philip Henslowe in 1594 and were on the bill at Court later that year over the Christmas season. The Chamberlain's Men main rival in London's theatre world was the Admiral's Men and between the two of them, they put on all theatrical performances in the city.

Lord Chamberlain's Men now had a base at the Shoreditch Theatre on the London side of the Thames River. This was an important factor for the rest of William's career – it now settled down to something of permanence. Shakespeare was an asset to the company – he brought in his body of work that could serve as part of the company's repertoire for years to come. William produced about two plays a year until he left London to live out his final days in Stratford.

The first Shakespeare play that was a success after the Plague years was *Richard III*, another history play that chronicled the downfall of the Plantagenet royal house and opened the door for the rise of the Tudor dynasty. No doubt this play was popularly supported by the monarch and her Court of the time. Three other well-regarded and often performed plays were thought to have been written during William's first years with the Chamberlain's Men – *A Midsummer Night's Dream*, *Romeo and Juliet*, *Love's Labour Lost*, and *Richard II*. The variety of comedy, tragedy, and history plays reflect Shakespeare's talent and versatility. Around this time Shakespeare garnered high praise from a fellow writer Francis Meres. Meres made reference to William's sonnets, which were not actually published for another eleven years.

Tragedy struck the Shakespeare family in 1596 when William and Anne's only son Hamnet. In 1597 William, obviously enjoying some material success with his writing career, purchased a larger house in Stratford, New Place, the second largest estate in the parish. Shakespeare still spent much of his time in London but as the years went on, he returned to Stratford more and more. The playwright was not only a creative type – he had a keen business sense, as well, or possibly good advisors. He invested in property, and by 1599 he was part owner of the Globe Theatre, forever afterward associated with Shakespeare.

After the Globe Theatre was built in 1599 Shakespeare became a prominent member of the King's Men – the company was sponsored by the King himself, James I, when he ascended the throne in 1603. The company was commanded to produce and perform plays "for our (the King's) solace and pleasure". Shakespeare produced a great body of work over the next ten years. The Globe burned down during a performance of Henry VIII (a fired canon caused the thatched roof to catch fire). No one was killed, and the Globe was rebuilt soon after. At about this time, after investing in the new theatre, Shakespeare retired to spend most of his time in Stratford. He died at New Place on his 52nd birthday. He was survived by his wife, two daughters, two sons-in-law, and a grandchild. His wife Anne outlived him, dying in 1623. One of the few official documentation of Shakepeare's to have survived is his will – in which he left his wife "his second-best bed" (by law, she would have also inherited one-third of his estate). William and Anne were survived by their two daughters, both married and who would leave descendants.

Modern Version of the Play

Characters

Brutus-Supporter of the Republic and friend of Caesar

Julius Caesar-Roman general and senator

Antony-Loyal Friend of Caesar

Cassius-General

Octavius-Caesar's adopted son

Casca-A representative and one of the conspirators

Calpurnia-Caesar's wife

Portia-Brutus's wife and daughter of Cato

Flavius and Marullus-Two representatives

Cicero-Roman senator

Lepidus-Third member of Antony and Octavius's coalition

Decius-Member of the conspiracy

Act I

Scene 1: Rome. A street.

Enter Flavius, Marullus and certain Commoners

Flavius

Hence! home, you idle creatures, get you home! Is this a holiday? What! know you not, Being mechanical, you ought not walk Upon a laboring day without the sign Of your profession?--Speak, what trade art thou?

Hey! Go home you lazy bums. Is this a holiday? What's going on? This is a work day. What is your occupation?

First Commoner

Why, sir, a carpenter.

I am a carpenter, sir.

Marullus

Where is thy leather apron and thy rule? What dost thou with thy best apparel on?-- You, sir; what trade are you?

Where are your leather apron and your ruler? What are you doing in your best clothes? What is your occupation, sir?

Second Commoner

Truly, sir, in respect of a fine workman, I am but, as you would say, a cobbler.

I am a cobbler, sir.

Marullus

But what trade art thou? Answer me directly.

But, what do you do? Answer me, honestly.

Second Commoner

A trade, sir, that, I hope, I may use with a safe conscience, which is indeed, sir, a mender of bad soles.

I mend bad soles, sir. That is my trade.

Marullus

What trade, thou knave? Thou naughty knave, what trade?

That's not a trade, you liar. What kind of trade do you do?

Second Commoner

Nay, I beseech you, sir, be not out with me; yet, if you be out, sir, I can mend you.

Please don't be angry, sir. I can show you.

Marullus

What mean'st thou by that? Mend me, thou saucy fellow!

What do you mean? Show me? Are you getting smart with me?

Second Commoner

Why, sir, cobble you.

I mean fix your shoes.

Flavius

Thou art a cobbler, art thou?

Oh, you are a shoe repairman.

Second Commoner

Truly, Sir, all that I live by is with the awl; I meddle with no tradesman's matters, nor women's matters, but with awl. I am indeed, sir, a surgeon to old shoes; when they are in great danger, I re-cover them. As proper men as ever trod upon neat's-leather have gone upon my handiwork.

Yes, sir. I live by the awl. I am not a political man. I am like a doctor to old shoes. I save their lives when they are in danger. I have mended many a proper man's shoes.

Flavius

But wherefore art not in thy shop today? Why dost thou lead these men about the streets?

Why are you not in your shop, today? Why are you leading these men around?

Second Commoner

Truly, sir, to wear out their shoes to get myself into more work. But indeed, sir, we make holiday to see Caesar and to rejoice in his triumph.

I am hoping to get more work for myself by wearing out their shoes. But, sir, we have all taken off work to see Caesar and celebrate his success.

Marullus

Wherefore rejoice? What conquest brings he home? What tributaries follow him to Rome, To grace in captive bonds his chariot wheels? You blocks, you stones, you worse than senseless things! O you hard hearts, you cruel men of Rome, Knew you not Pompey? Many a time and oft Have you climb'd up to walls and battlements, To towers and windows, yea, to chimney tops, Your infants in your arms, and there have sat The livelong day with patient expectation To see great Pompey pass the streets of Rome. And when you saw his chariot but appear, Have you not made an universal shout That Tiber trembled underneath her banks To hear the replication of your sounds Made in her concave shores? And do you now put on your best attire? And do you now cull out a holiday? And do you now strew flowers in his way That comes in triumph over Pompey's blood? Be gone! Run to your houses, fall upon your knees, Pray to the gods to intermit the plague That needs must light on this ingratitude.

What is he celebrating? What has he done to receive such adoration? You idiots! Once, you did whatever you could to cheer on Pompey as he rode through the city of Rome. Now, you put on your best clothes and take off work to celebrate Pompey's murderer. Go home and pray to the gods to keep the plague away you deserve for such a showing of ingratitude.

Flavius

Go, go, good countrymen, and, for this fault, Assemble all the poor men of your sort, Draw them to Tiber banks, and weep your tears Into the channel, till the lowest stream Do kiss the most exalted shores of all.

Go on my fellow countrymen, and to make amends for your wrongdoings, go to the river Tiber and cry until its banks overflow.

Exit all the Commoners.

See whether their basest metal be not moved; They vanish tongue-tied in their guiltiness. Go you down that way towards the Capitol; This way will I. Disrobe the images, If you do find them deck'd with ceremonies.

Look at those morons leaving, speechless. Let's go down towards the Capitol and take the decorations from the statues.

Marullus

May we do so? You know it is the feast of Lupercal.

Can we do that? You know it is the feast of Lupercal.

Flavius

It is no matter; let no images Be hung with Caesar's trophies. I'll about And drive away the vulgar from the streets; So do you too, where you perceive them thick. These growing feathers pluck'd from Caesar's wing Will make him fly an ordinary pitch, Who else would soar above the view of men, And keep us all in servile fearfulness.

It doesn't matter. I don't want any of the statues decorated for Caesar. Make sure you disperse any of the crowds. If we take away his supporters, maybe he will be more realistic and start treating us fairly, instead of using fear.

Exit.

Scene II: A public place.

Flourish. Enter Caesar. Antony, for the course. Calpurnia, Portia, Decius Brutus, Cicero, Brutus, Cassius, and Casca. A great crowd following, among them a soothsayer.

Caesar

Calpurnia,--

Calpurnia!

Casca

Peace, ho! Caesar speaks.

Be quiet, everyone! Caesar speaks.

Caesar

Calpurnia,--

Calpurnia!

Calpurnia

Here, my lord.

Here I am, my lord.

Caesar

Stand you directly in Antonius' way, When he doth run his course.--Antonius,--

You are standing in Antony's way when he runs the race. Antony

Antony

Caesar, my lord?

Yes, my lord?

Caesar

Forget not in your speed, Antonius, To touch Calpurnia; for our elders say, The barren, touched in this holy chase, Shake off their sterile curse.

Don't forget to touch Calpurnia when you begin to race. The old men say if a childless woman is touched in this holy race, she'll become fertile.

Antony

I shall remember. When Caesar says "Do this," it is perform'd.

I won't forget. When you tell me to do something, it is as good as done.

Caesar

Set on; and leave no ceremony out.

Okay, then. Get going, and don't leave out any rituals.

Flourish

Soothsayer

Caesar!

Caesar!

Caesar

Ha! Who calls?

Who's calling me?

Casca

Bid every noise be still.--Peace yet again!

Be quiet everyone!

Caesar

Who is it in the press that calls on me? I hear a tongue, shriller than all the music, Cry "Caesar"! Speak, Caesar is turn'd to hear.

Who's calling me? I hear a shrill voice over the music crying, "Caesar!" Speak, I'm listening.

Soothsayer

Beware the Ides of March.

Beware the ides of March.

Caesar

What man is that?

Who is that?

Brutus

A soothsayer bids you beware the Ides of March.

A soothsayer is telling you to beware of March 15th.

Caesar

Set him before me; let me see his face.

Bring him to me. I want to see his face.

Cassius

Fellow, come from the throng; look upon Caesar.

Fellow, come out of the crowd. Look at Caesar.

Soothsayer approaches.

Caesar

What say'st thou to me now? Speak once again.

What do you want to say to me now? Speak again.

Soothsayer

Beware the Ides of March.

Beware of March 15th.

Caesar

He is a dreamer; let us leave him. Pass.

He's crazy. Let's leave.

Exit all except Brutus and Cassius.

Cassius

Will you go see the order of the course?

Are you going to watch the race?

Brutus

Not I

No, not me.

Cassius

I pray you, do.

Oh, please do.

Brutus

I am not gamesome; I do lack some part Of that quick spirit that is in Antony. Let me not hinder, Cassius, your desires; I'll leave you.

I don't care for sports like Antony, but don't let me stop you, Cassius. I'll leave.

Cassius

Brutus, I do observe you now of late: I have not from your eyes that gentleness And show of love as I was wont to have: You bear too stubborn and too strange a hand Over your friend that loves you.

Brutus, I have observed lately that you don't seem to have the same feelings towards me, you once had. You have been stubborn and unfriendly to me, your friend who loves you.

Brutus

Cassius, Be not deceived: if I have veil'd my look, I turn the trouble of my countenance Merely upon myself. Vexed I am Of late with passions of some difference, Conceptions only proper to myself, Which give some soil perhaps to my behaviors; But let not therefore my good friends be grieved-- Among which number, Cassius, be you one-- Nor construe any further my neglect, Than that poor Brutus, with himself at war, Forgets the shows of love to other men.

Cassius, don't be fooled. If I have looked differently lately, it has nothing to do with you. I have been preoccupied with personal affairs. So, don't worry about our relationship. Just know, that I am at war with myself and haven't been myself.

Cassius

Then, Brutus, I have much mistook your passion; By means whereof this breast of mine hath buried Thoughts of great value, worthy cogitations. Tell me, good Brutus, can you see your face?

Well then, let me tell you I have been keeping some very interesting thoughts to myself. Brutus, can you see your face?

Brutus

No, Cassius, for the eye sees not itself But by reflection, by some other thing.

No, Cassius, the eye cannot see itself, except in its reflection.

Cassius

'Tis just: And it is very much lamented, Brutus, That you have no such mirrors as will turn Your hidden worthiness into your eye, That you might see your shadow. I have heard Where many of the best respect in Rome,-- Except immortal Caesar!-- speaking of Brutus, And groaning underneath this age's yoke, Have wish'd that noble Brutus had his eyes.

True, but that's too bad. I wish you could see what others think about you. Many respect you almost as much as Caesar. They wish you could do something about the tyranny of today's government.

Brutus

Into what dangers would you lead me, Cassius, That you would have me seek into myself For that which is not in me?

Cassius, to what are you alluding? It sounds like something dangerous. I don't have it in me.

Cassius

Therefore, good Brutus, be prepared to hear; And since you know you cannot see yourself So well as by reflection, I, your glass, Will modestly discover to yourself That of yourself which you yet know not of. And be not jealous on me, gentle Brutus; Were I a common laugher, or did use To stale with ordinary oaths my love To every new protester; if you know That I do fawn on men, and hug them hard And after scandal them; or if you know That I profess myself, in banqueting, To all the rout, then hold me dangerous.

Good Brutus, listen to what I have to say. Let me be your mirror. If you don't believe me to be genuine in my observations, then consider me dangerous.

Flourish, and shouts.

Brutus

What means this shouting? I do fear the people Choose Caesar for their king.

What does the shouting mean? I am afraid the people choose Caesar for king.

Cassius

Ay, do you fear it? Then must I think you would not have it so.

You fear it? Then, I must believe you would have it otherwise.

Brutus

I would not, Cassius; yet I love him well, But wherefore do you hold me here so long? What is it that you would impart to me? If it be aught toward the general good, Set honor in one eye and death i' the other And I will look on both indifferently; For let the gods so speed me as I love The name of honor more than I fear death.

I wouldn't, Cassius. I love him very much. So, what do you want to tell me? What is so important? If it is good for everyone, then I will listen even if it means death. I love honor more than I fear death.

Cassius

I know that virtue to be in you, Brutus, As well as I do know your outward favor. Well, honor is the subject of my story. I cannot tell what you and other men Think of this life; but, for my single self, I had as lief not be as live to be In awe of such a thing as I myself. I was born free as Caesar; so were you: We both have fed as well; and we can both Endure the winter's cold as well as he: For once, upon a raw and gusty day, The troubled Tiber chafing with her shores, Caesar said to me, "Darest thou, Cassius, now Leap in with me into this angry flood And swim to yonder point?" Upon the word, Accoutred as I was, I plunged in, And bade him follow: so indeed he did. The torrent roar'd, and we did buffet it With lusty sinews, throwing it aside And stemming it with hearts of controversy; But ere we could arrive the point proposed, Caesar cried, "Help me, Cassius, or I sink! I, as Aeneas, our great ancestor, Did from the flames of Troy upon his shoulder The old Anchises bear, so from the waves of Tiber Did I the tired Caesar: and this man Is now become a god; and Cassius is A wretched creature, and must bend his body, If Caesar carelessly but nod on him. He had a fever when he was in Spain; And when the fit was on him I did mark How he did shake: 'tis true, this god did shake: His coward lips did from their color fly; And that same eye whose bend doth awe the world Did lose his luster. I did hear him groan: Ay, and that tongue of his that bade the Romans Mark him, and write his speeches in their books, Alas, it cried, "Give me some drink, Titinius," As a sick girl.--Ye gods, it doth amaze me, A man of such a feeble temper should So get the start of the majestic world, And bear the palm alone.

I know you are honorable, Brutus. I also know you are loyal to Caesar. But, my point is honor. I cannot speak for other men, but for me, I cannot live worshiping a man no more special than myself. Both Caesar and I were born free men. We were friends, once, and I saved his life in the river Tiber. I have also seen him cry out like a sick little girl when we were in Spain. Now, he is looked upon as if he was a god, and I am a mere worker.

Shout. Flourish.

Brutus

Another general shout! I do believe that these applauses are For some new honors that are heap'd on Caesar.

There's another shout. I believe they are for Caesar.

Cassius

Why, man, he doth bestride the narrow world Like a Colossus; and we petty men Walk under his huge legs and peep about To find ourselves dishonorable graves. Men at some time are masters of their fates: The fault, dear

Brutus, is not in our stars, But in ourselves,that we are underlings. "Brutus" and "Caesar": what should be in that "Caesar"? Why should that name be sounded more than yours? Write them together, yours is as fair a name; Sound them, it doth become the mouth as well; Weigh them, it is as heavy; conjure with them, "Brutus" will start a spirit as soon as "Caesar." Now, in the names of all the gods at once, Upon what meat doth this our Caesar feed That he is grown so great? Age, thou art shamed! Rome, thou hast lost the breed of noble bloods! When went there by an age since the great flood, But it was famed with more than with one man? When could they say, till now, that talk'd of Rome, That her wide walls encompass'd but one man? Now is it Rome indeed, and room enough, When there is in it but one only man. O, you and I have heard our fathers say There was a Brutus once that would have brook'd Th' eternal devil to keep his state in Rome, As easily as a king!

He does walk around the world like a giant, while we petty men walk under his huge legs and look around until we are in our graves. Men may be the masters of their own fates, but sometimes they do themselves an injustice. Why should Caesar be any more important than you? Your name is just as good as his. They are both easy to say. What makes him better than you? What has happened to Rome? Once, Rome bred many great men. Now, it seems there is only room for one. You know what our ancestors said. They would have let the devil rule Rome before a king.

Brutus

That you do love me, I am nothing jealous; What you would work me to, I have some aim: How I have thought of this, and of these times, I shall recount hereafter; for this present, I would not, so with love I might entreat you, Be any further moved. What you have said, I will consider; what you have to say, I will with patience hear; and find a time Both meet to hear and answer such high things. Till then, my noble friend, chew upon this: Brutus had rather be a villager Than to repute himself a son of Rome Under these hard conditions as this time Is like to lay upon us.

I know you love me, but I am not jealous. I think I know what you want me to do. I have thought of this before, but for now, I ask that you say no more. Listen to me. I had rather be a nobody than a Roman living in these conditions.

Cassius

I am glad that my weak words Have struck but thus much show of fire from Brutus.

I am glad my simple words have moved you.

Brutus

The games are done, and Caesar is returning.

The race is over and Caesar is coming back.

Cassius

As they pass by, pluck Casca by the sleeve; And he will, after his sour fashion, tell you What hath proceeded worthy note today.

As the crowd passes by, get Casca's attention. He will tell you what happened today.

Re-enter Caesar and his Train.

Brutus

I will do so.--But, look you, Cassius, The angry spot doth glow on Caesar's brow, And all the rest look like a chidden train: Calpurnia's cheek is pale; and Cicero Looks with such ferret and such fiery eyes As we have seen him in the Capitol, Being cross'd in conference by some senators.

I will, but look, Cassius. Caesar looks angry and the rest look like a broken train. Calpurnia looks pale and Cicero looks angry, like he does in the Capitol when senators disagree with him.

Cassius

Casca will tell us what the matter is.

Casca will tell us what's going on.

Caesar

Antonius,--

Antony!

Antony

Caesar?

Caesar?

Caesar

Let me have men about me that are fat; Sleek-headed men, and such as sleep o' nights: Yond Cassius has a lean and hungry look; He thinks too much: such men are dangerous.

Surround me with fat, lazy men. See Cassius over there. He has a hungry look about him, and he thinks too much. Men, like him, are dangerous.

Antony

Fear him not, Caesar; he's not dangerous; He is a noble Roman and well given.

You needn't fear him. He's not dangerous. He is a well-known and noble Roman.

Caesar

Would he were fatter! But I fear him not: Yet, if my name were liable to fear, I do not know the man I should avoid So soon as that spare Cassius. He reads much; He is a great observer, and he looks Quite through the deeds of men: he loves no plays, As thou dost, Antony; he hears no music: Seldom he smiles; and smiles in such a sort As if he mock'd himself and scorn'd his spirit That could be moved to smile at any thing. Such men as he be never at heart's ease Whiles they behold a greater than themselves; And therefore are they very dangerous. I rather tell thee what is to be fear'd Than what I fear, for always I am Caesar. Come on my right hand, for this ear is deaf, And tell me truly what thou think'st of him.

I don't fear him, but I wish he were fatter! Cassius, if I were fearful, is the kind of man one should fear. He is well-read and watches everything closely. He has no joys, like plays or music. He rarely smiles, and if he does it's at something he said. Men, like Cassius, are never at ease, especially around someone greater than themselves. Therefore, they are dangerous. I am just telling you what should be feared; not what I fear, for I am Caesar. Now, come on my right side, because my left ear is deaf and tell me what you think of him.

Trumpets play. Caesar exits with all his followers except Casca.

Casca

You pull'd me by the cloak; would you speak with me?

You tugged on my sleeve. Do you want to speak with me?

Brutus

Ay, Casca, tell us what hath chanced today, That Caesar looks so sad.

Yes, Casca. Tell us what happened today that made Caesar look so sad.

Casca

Why, you were with him, were you not?

Why? Weren't you with him?

Brutus

I should not then ask Casca what had chanced.

I wouldn't have asked if I were.

Casca

Why, there was a crown offer'd him; and being offer'd him, he put it by with the back of his hand, thus; and then the people fell a-shouting.

Someone offered him a crown and he pushed it aside with the back of his hand, like this. Then, the people started shouting.

Brutus

What was the second noise for?

What was the second shout for?

Casca

Why, for that too.

Same thing.

Cassius

They shouted thrice: what was the last cry for?

They shouted three times. What was the last cry for?

Casca

Why, for that too.

Same reason as the first two.

Brutus

Was the crown offer'd him thrice?

Was the crown offered to him three times?

Casca

Ay, marry, was't, and he put it by thrice, every time gentler than other; and at every putting-by mine honest neighbors shouted.

Yes and each time he turned it down gently, and the crowds started shouting.

Cassius

Who offer'd him the crown?

Who offered him the crown?

Casca

Why, Antony.

Antony.

Brutus

Tell us the manner of it, gentle Casca.

Tell us how it happened.

Casca

I can as well be hang'd, as tell the manner of it: it was mere foolery; I did not mark it. I saw Mark Antony offer him a crown;--yet 'twas not a crown neither, 'twas one of these coronets;--and, as I told you, he put it by once: but, for all that, to my thinking, he would fain have had it. Then he offered it to him again: then he put it by again: but, to my thinking, he was very loath to lay his fingers off it. And then he offered it the third time; he put it the third time by; and still, as he refused it, the rabblement shouted, and clapp'd their chopt hands, and threw up their sweaty night-caps, and uttered such a deal of stinking breath because Caesar refused the crown, that it had almost choked Caesar, for he swooned and fell down at it: and for mine own part, I durst not laugh for fear of opening my lips and receiving the bad air.

I just as soon be hanged as to tell it, it was so foolish. I didn't pay much attention. I saw Mark Antony offer him a crown. It was really just one of those head pieces. Anyway, Caesar turned it down, although I thought he wanted it. Then, Antony offered it to him again, and he pushed it away, but this time his hand stayed on it longer. Then, the third time Antony offered it the crowd went wild throwing up their sweaty hats and yelling that Caesar passed out. As for myself, I didn't dare laugh, for fear of breathing in the stench.

Cassius

But, soft! I pray you. What, did Caesar swoon?

Tell us again. Did you say Caesar fainted?

Casca

He fell down in the market-place, and foam'd at mouth, and was speechless.

He fell down in the market-place and began foaming at the mouth. He couldn't even speak.

Brutus

'Tis very like: he hath the falling-sickness.

Sounds like he has the falling sickness.

Cassius

No, Caesar hath it not; but you, and I, And honest Casca, we have the falling-sickness.

No, Caesar doesn't have it, but we do.

Casca

I know not what you mean by that; but I am sure Caesar fell down. If the tag-rag people did not clap him and hiss him, according as he pleased and displeased them, as they use to do the players in the theatre, I am no true man.

I don't know what you mean, but I am telling the truth. The crowd responded to him in pleasure and displeasure, just like they do in the theater.

Brutus

What said he when he came unto himself?

What did he say when he came around?

Casca

Marry, before he fell down, when he perceived the common herd was glad he refused the crown, he pluck'd me ope his doublet, and offered them his throat to cut: an I had been a man of any occupation, if I would not have taken him at a word, I would I might go to hell among the rogues:--and so he fell. When he came to himself again, he said, if he had done or said any thing amiss, he desired their worships to think it was his infirmity. Three or four wenches where I stood cried, "Alas, good soul!" and forgave him with all their hearts. But there's no heed to be taken of them: if Caesar had stabb'd their mothers, they would have done no less.

Before he fell, he opened up his robe and offered them his throat to cut. If I were a different man, I might go to hell with that offer. Then, he fainted. When he came back around, he said it was just his illness. Three or four women by me cried, "Ah, poor soul!" But, they would have done that if Caesar had just stabbed their mothers.

Brutus

And, after that he came, thus sad away?

And after that, he came back looking so sad?

Casca

Ay.

Yes.

Cassius

Did Cicero say any thing?

Did Cicero say anything?

Casca

Ay, he spoke Greek.

Yes, he spoke in Greek.

Cassius

To what effect?

What did he say?

Casca

Nay, an I tell you that, I'll ne'er look you i' the face again: but those that understood him smiled at one another and shook their heads; but for mine own part, it was Greek to me. I could tell you more news too: Marullus and Flavius, for pulling scarfs off Caesar's images, are put to silence. Fare you well. There was more foolery yet, if could remember it.

I don't know. It was all Greek to me, but I can tell you those who understood him were smiling and shaking their heads. Also, Marullus and Flavius were punished for taking the decorations off the statues of Caesar. There was some more foolishness, but I can't remember.

Cassius

Will you sup with me tonight, Casca?

Will you have dinner with me tonight, Casca?

Casca

No, I am promised forth.

No, I already have plans.

Cassius

Will you dine with me tomorrow?

How about tomorrow night?

Casca

Ay, if I be alive, and your mind hold, and your dinner worth the eating.

Yes, if I'm alive and you still will have me and of course if the food's any good.

Cassius

Good; I will expect you.

Good, I'll be expecting you.

Casca

Do so; farewell both.

You do that. Goodbye, fellows.

Exit

Brutus

What a blunt fellow is this grown to be! He was quick mettle when he went to school.

What a forward guy he has become! He was always so shy in school.

Cassius

So is he now in execution Of any bold or noble enterprise, However he puts on this tardy form. This rudeness is a sauce to his good wit, Which gives men stomach to digest his words With better appetite.

He's smart though, even if he plays stupid. He comes across as abrasive, but it's just a way to get people to listen to him.

Brutus

And so it is. For this time I will leave you: Tomorrow, if you please to speak with me, I will come home to you; or, if you will, Come home to me, and I will wait for you.

You're probably right. I've got to go, though. If you want to talk tomorrow, you can come to my house, or I will go to yours.

Cassius

I will do so: till then, think of the world.--

Sounds good. Till then, think about the world.

Exit Brutus.

Well, Brutus, thou art noble; yet, I see, Thy honorable metal may be wrought, From that it is disposed: therefore 'tis meet That noble minds keep ever with their likes; For who so firm that cannot be seduced? Caesar doth bear me hard, but he loves Brutus; If I were Brutus now and he were Cassius, He should not humor me. I will this night, In several hands, in at his windows throw, As if they came from several citizens, Writings all tending to the great opinion That Rome holds of his name; wherein obscurely Caesar's ambition shall be glanced at: And after this let Caesar seat him sure; For we will shake him, or worse days endure.

Well, Brutus, you are noble, but not so noble that you can't be swayed. That's why we must stick together. Caesar may not like me, but he loves Brutus. Now, if I was Brutus and he was me, he wouldn't have listened to me tonight. So, I will write several letters in different handwriting to disguise their true sender to convey the feelings of Rome; Brutus is loved and Caesar is too ambitious. After that, let's see how long Caesar keeps his throne or worse.

Exit.

Scene III: The same. A street.

Thunder and lightning. Enter Casca with his sword drawn opposite of Cicero.

Cicero

Good even, Casca: brought you Caesar home? Why are you breathless, and why stare you so?

Good evening, Casca. Are you coming from Caesar's house? Why are you breathless and bewildered?

Casca

Are not you moved, when all the sway of earth Shakes like a thing unfirm? O Cicero, I have seen tempests, when the scolding winds Have rived the knotty oaks; and I have seen Th' ambitious ocean swell and rage and foam, To be exalted with the threatening clouds: But never till tonight, never till now, Did I go through a tempest dropping fire. Either there is a civil strife in heaven, Or else the world too saucy with the gods, Incenses them to send destruction.

Aren't you moved when all of the earth is shaking? Oh Cicero, I have seen storms when the winds broke old oak trees and I have seen the ocean swell and rage with foam, but I have never seen a storm that dropped fire like rain. Not until tonight, not until now. Either there is a storm in heaven or the world is about to come to an end.

Cicero

Why, saw you anything more wonderful?

What have you seen so strange?

Casca

A common slave--you'd know him well by sight-- Held up his left hand, which did flame and burn Like twenty torches join'd, and yet his hand Not sensible of fire remain'd unscorch'd. Besides,--I ha' not since put up my sword,-- Against the Capitol I met a lion, Who glared upon me, and went surly by, Without annoying me: and there were drawn Upon a heap a hundred ghastly women, Transformed with their fear; who swore they saw Men, all in fire, walk up and down the streets. And yesterday the bird of night did sit Even at noonday upon the marketplace, Howling and shrieking. When these prodigies Do so conjointly meet, let not men say "These are their reasons; they are natural"; For I believe they are portentous things Unto the climate that they point upon.

I saw a familiar slave hold up his hand. It was on fire, but it didn't get burned. Then, when I took out my sword, I saw a lion that looked at me but didn't attack. Later, there were a hundred women who swore they saw men on fire walking down the streets. Yesterday, the night owl was I the marketplace hooting at noon. When these things take place, we must pay attention. They are an omen of bad things to come.

Cicero

Indeed, it is a strange-disposed time. But men may construe things after their fashion, Clean from the purpose of the things themselves. Comes Caesar to the Capitol tomorrow?

That is certainly strange, but men sometimes see things they want to see that aren't actually correct. Is Caesar coming to the Capitol tomorrow?

Casca

He doth, for he did bid Antonius Send word to you he would be there to-morrow.

He is because he told Antony to tell you he would be there tomorrow.

Cicero

Good then, Casca: this disturbed sky Is not to walk in.

Good night then, Cicero. This is not a good night to walk around according to the sky.

Exit Cicero.

Enter Cassius.

Cassius

Who's there?

Who's there?

Casca

A Roman.

A Roman.

Cassius

Casca, by your voice.

I recognize your voice, Casca.

Casca

Your ear is good. Cassius, what night is this!

You've got a good ear, Cassius! What a night this has been!

Cassius

A very pleasing night to honest men.

It has been a good night for honest men.

Casca

Who ever knew the heavens menace so?

Who knew the heavens could be so menacing?

Cassius

Those that have known the earth so full of faults. For my part, I have walk'd about the streets, Submitting me unto the perilous night; And, thus unbraced, Casca, as you see, Have bared my bosom to the thunder-stone; And when the cross blue lightning seem'd to open The breast of heaven, I did present myself Even in the aim and very flash of it.

Those that have known the earth's faults, like me. I walked about the streets welcoming the thunder and the lightning.

Casca

But wherefore did you so much tempt the Heavens? It is the part of men to fear and tremble, When the most mighty gods by tokens send Such dreadful heralds to astonish us.

Why would you tempt the heavens like that? Most men would tremble with fear when the gods send us such astonishing sights.

Cassius

You are dull, Casca;and those sparks of life That should be in a Roman you do want, Or else you use not. You look pale and gaze, And put on fear and cast yourself in wonder, To see the strange impatience of the Heavens: But if you would consider the true cause Why all these fires, why all these gliding ghosts, Why birds and beasts,from quality and kind; Why old men, fools, and children calculate;-- Why all these things change from their ordinance, Their natures, and preformed faculties To monstrous quality;--why, you shall find That Heaven hath infused them with these spirits, To make them instruments of fear and warning Unto some monstrous state. Now could I, Casca, Name to thee a man most like this dreadful night; That thunders, lightens, opens graves, and roars, As doth the lion in the Capitol; A man no mightier than thyself or me In personal action; yet prodigious grown, And fearful, as these strange eruptions are.

You are dumb, Casca. You lack the characteristics of a Roman, or else you aren't showing them. If you think about all of these strange occurrences, you would realize, it's the gods foreshadowing some awful things to come. Right now, I can think of an ordinary man in the Capitol who, like these strange occurrences, performs unbelievable acts.

Casca

'Tis Caesar that you mean; is it not, Cassius?

You're talking about Caesar, aren't you, Cassius?

Cassius

Let it be who it is: for Romans now Have thews and limbs like to their ancestors; But, woe the while! our fathers' minds are dead, And we are govern'd with our mothers' spirits; Our yoke and sufferance show us womanish.

Whoever. We may look like our Roman forefathers, but we are acting like our mothers.

Casca

Indeed they say the senators to-morrow Mean to establish Caesar as a king; And he shall wear his crown by sea and land, In every place save here in Italy.

True. They say the senators are planning on making Caesar king, tomorrow. He will wear his crown everywhere, except here in Italy.

Cassius

I know where I will wear this dagger then; Cassius from bondage will deliver Cassius: Therein, ye gods, you make the weak most strong; Therein, ye gods, you tyrants do defeat: Nor stony tower, nor walls of beaten brass, Nor airless dungeon, nor strong links of iron Can be retentive to the strength of spirit; But life, being weary of these worldly bars, Never lacks power to dismiss itself. If I know this, know all the world besides, That part of tyranny that I do bear I can shake off at pleasure.

I know where this dagger will be worn, then. I will not be reined. Nothing can deter me, not even death. Let everyone know that I can shake off the threat of tyranny, when I want.

Thunder continues.

Casca

So can I: So every bondman in his own hand bears The power to cancel his captivity.

So can I. Every man has the strength to overcome bondage.

Cassius

And why should Caesar be a tyrant then? Poor man! I know he would not be a wolf, But that he sees the Romans are but sheep: He were no lion, were not Romans hinds. Those that with haste will make a mighty fire Begin it with weak straws: what trash is Rome, What rubbish, and what offal, when it serves For the base matter to illuminate So vile a thing as Caesar! But, O grief, Where hast thou led me? I perhaps speak this Before a willing bondman: then I know My answer must be made; but I am arm'd, And dangers are to me indifferent.

Poor Caesar! He thinks Romans are sheep and he is a wolf. He wouldn't be a lion, if Rome weren't acting like a bunch of donkeys. People, who want to make a big fire, start with little sticks. Rome has become complete trash, the way it adores Caesar. But, wait, I may be talking to someone who wants to be a slave. Then, I may be in danger for what I'm saying. It doesn't matter because I am armed and not afraid.

Casca

You speak to Casca; and to such a man That is no fleering tell-tale. Hold, my hand: Be factious for redress of all these griefs; And I will set this foot of mine as far As who goes farthest.

Hey, you're talking to me. I'm not two-faced. I won't tell anyone. Let's shake and join together to right these wrongs. I will go as far as any man.

Cassius

There's a bargain made. Now know you, Casca, I have moved already Some certain of the noblest-minded

Romans To undergo with me an enterprise Of honorable-dangerous consequence; And I do know by this, they stay for me In Pompey's Porch: for now, this fearful night, There is no stir or walking in the streets; And the complexion of the element Is favor'd like the work we have in hand, Most bloody, fiery, and most terrible.

That's a deal. Now, I must tell you, I have already been working on some of the noblest minds in Rome to join with me in overthrowing Caesar. But, it's going to be dangerous, so we are meeting tonight at Pompey's porch because no one will be out in this weather.

Casca

Stand close awhile, for here comes one in haste.

Hang on. Here comes someone now.

Cassius

'Tis Cinna; I do know him by his gait; He is a friend.--

It's Cinna. I recognize his walk. He is a friend.

Enter Cinna

Cinna, where haste you so?

Cinna, where are you going in such a hurry?

Cinna

To find out you. Who's that? Metellus Cimber?

To find you. Who's that? Metellus Cimber?

Cassius

No, it is Casca, one incorporate To our attempts. Am I not stay'd for, Cinna?

No, it's Casca. He is one of us. Are the others ready?

Cinna

I am glad on't. What a fearful night is this! There's two or three of us have seen strange sights.

Good, I'm glad. This has been a scary night. There are a couple of guys who have seen some strange sights.

Cassius

Am I not stay'd for? tell me.

Have the people gathered? Tell me.

Cinna

Yes, You are. O Cassius, if you could but win The noble Brutus to our party,--

Yes, they are. Please bring Brutus to join us.

Cassius

Be you content. Good Cinna, take this paper, And look you lay it in the praetor's chair, Where Brutus may but find it; and throw this In at his window; set this up with wax Upon old Brutus' statue: all this done, Repair to Pompey's Porch, where you shall find us. Is Decius Brutus and Trebonius there?

Be patient, good Cinna. Take this paper and put it in the chair where Brutus sits, throw this in his window, and put this on old Brutus's statue. When you have done all this, go to the theater where we will be. Are Decius Brutus and Trebonius there?

Cinna

All but Metellus Cimber, and he's gone To seek you at your house. Well, I will hie And so bestow these papers as you bade me.

Everyone is there but Metellus Cimber. He's gone to your house looking for you. Well, I'll go deliver these papers as you wish.

Cassius

That done, repair to Pompey's theatre.--

When you're done, go to Pompey's theater.

Exit Cinna.

Come, Casca, you and I will yet, ere day, See Brutus at his house: three parts of him Is ours already; and the man entire, Upon the next encounter, yields him ours.

Come on, Casca. You and I will go to Brutus's house. He is three-fourths ours, and I bet after our visit we will have him completely.

Casca

O, he sits high in all the people's hearts! And that which would appear offense in us, His countenance, like richest alchemy, Will change to virtue and to worthiness.

The people love him. So, with him we can do no wrong in their eyes.

Cassius

Him, and his worth, and our great need of him, You have right well conceited. Let us go, For it is after midnight; and, ere day, We will awake him, and be sure of him.

You are so right. We need him. Let's go for it's almost midnight. We will wake him up.

Exit.

Act II

Scene I: Rome. Brutus's orchard.

Enter Brutus.

Brutus

What, Lucius, ho!-- I cannot, by the progress of the stars, Give guess how near to day.--Lucius, I say!-- I would it were my fault to sleep so soundly.-- When, Lucius, when! Awake, I say! What, Lucius!

What's going on, Lucius? What time is it? I say, Lucius! I can't believe I slept so soundly. Wake up, Lucius! What time is it? Lucius!

Enter Lucius

Lucius

Call'd you, my lord?

Did you call, my lord?

Brutus

Get me a taper in my study, Lucius: When it is lighted, come and call me here.

Bring a candle to my study, Lucius, and when it is lit, call me.

Lucius

I will, my lord.

I will, my lord.

Exit.

Brutus

It must be by his death: and, for my part, I know no personal cause to spurn at him, But for the general. He would be crown'd: How that might change his nature, there's the question: It is the bright day that brings forth the adder; And that craves wary walking. Crown him?--that: And then, I grant, we put a sting in him, That at his will he may do danger with. Th' abuse of greatness is, when it disjoins Remorse from power; and, to speak truth of Caesar, I have not known when his affections sway'd More than his reason. But 'tis a common proof, That lowliness is young ambition's ladder, Whereto the climber-upward turns his face; But, when he once attains the upmost round, He then unto the ladder turns his back, Looks in the clouds, scorning the base degrees By which he did ascend: so Caesar may; Then, lest he may, prevent. And, since the quarrel Will bear no color for the thing he is, Fashion it thus,--that what he is, augmented, Would run to these and these extremities: And therefore think him as a serpent's egg Which hatch'd, would, as his kind grow mischievous; And kill him in the shell.

If Caesar wants to be crowned, despite what may happen, what part do I play? I have no reason to want his death, but Rome's best interest is at hand. I wonder if it will change his nature. Everyone knows that when one climbs the ladder of success and reaches the top rung, the climber's back is turned on everyone below him. Caesar may become high-minded and power-hungry. If so, his life must be taken.

Re-enter Lucius.

Lucius

The taper burneth in your closet, sir. Searching the window for a flint I found This paper thus seal'd up, and I am sure It did not lie there when I went to bed.

The candle is lit in your study, sir. While I was looking for the flint, I found this sealed letter. I'm sure it wasn't there earlier.

Brutus

Get you to bed again; it is not day. Is not tomorrow, boy, the Ides of March?

Go to bed, now. Isn't tomorrow the Ides of March?

Lucius

I know not, sir.

I don't know, sir.

Brutus

Look in the calendar, and bring me word.

Look in the calendar, and let me know.

Lucius

I will, sir.

I will, sir.

Exit.

Brutus

The exhalations, whizzing in the air Give so much light that I may read by them.--

[Opens the letter and reads.] "Brutus, thou sleep'st: awake and see thyself. Shall Rome, &c. Speak, strike, redress--! Brutus, thou sleep'st: awake!--"

Such instigations have been often dropp'd Where I have took them up. "Shall Rome, & c." Thus must I piece it out: Shall Rome stand under one man's awe? What, Rome? My ancestors did from the streets of Rome The Tarquin drive, when he was call'd a king.-- "Speak, strike, redress!"--Am I entreated, then, To speak and strike? O Rome, I make thee promise, If the redress will follow, thou receivest Thy full petition at the hand of Brutus!

The sky is lit by stars and meteors so, I may read this letter.

Opens the letter and reads.

"Brutus, You are asleep. Wake up and see what is happening to Rome. Speak, strike, help us! Brutus, you are asleep. Wake up and take action. What is going to happen to Rome? Should it be ruled by one man? Our ancestors drove off King Tarquin. Speak, strike, help!" Am I supposed to speak and strike. Oh, Rome, I promise you I will help protect you.

Re-enter Lucius.

Lucius

Sir, March is wasted fifteen days.

Tomorrow is March fourteenth.

Knocking within.

Brutus

'Tis good. Go to the gate, somebody knocks.--

Good. Go the gate and see who is knocking.

Exit Lucius.

Since Cassius first did whet me against Caesar I have not slept. Between the acting of a dreadful thing And the first motion, all the interim is Like a phantasma or a hideous dream: The genius and the mortal instruments Are then in council; and the state of man, Like to a little kingdom, suffers then The nature of an insurrection.

Since Cassius first told me he wants me to go against Caesar, I haven't slept. My mind has been filled with thought of taking action against the General. My body and my mind are in turmoil.

Re-enter Lucius.

Lucius

Sir, 'tis your brother Cassius at the door, Who doth desire to see you.

Sir, it's your brother, Cassius, at the door. He wants to see you.

Brutus

Is he alone?

Is he by himself?

Lucius

No, sir, there are more with him.

No, sir. More men are with him.

Brutus

Do you know them?

Do you know any of them?

Lucius

No, sir, their hats are pluck'd about their ears, And half their faces buried in their cloaks, That by no means I may discover them By any mark of favor.

I can't see their faces because their hats are pulled down and their faces are half buried in their coats.

Brutus

Let 'em enter.--

Let them come in.

Exit Lucius.

They are the faction.--O conspiracy, Shamest thou to show thy dangerous brow by night, When evils are most free? O, then, by day Where wilt thou find a cavern dark enough To mask thy monstrous visage? Seek none, conspiracy; Hide it in smiles and affability: For if thou pass, thy native semblance on, Not Erebus itself were dim enough To hide thee from prevention.

They are the conspirators. Only dangerous activities take place by night, when evil is most free. In the day, how will they continue to hide their plans. If they showed their true plans, hell would not be able to hide them from being found.

Enter the conspirators, Cassius, Casca, Decius Brutus, Cinna, Metellus Cimber, and Trebonius.

Cassius

I think we are too bold upon your rest: Good morrow, Brutus; do we trouble you?

Are we bothering you, Brutus? We are probably disturbing your rest. Good night.

Brutus

I have been up this hour, awake all night. Know I these men that come along with you?

I have been up and awake all night. Do I know your companions?

Cassius

Yes, every man of them; and no man here But honors you; and every one doth wish You had but that opinion of yourself Which every noble Roman bears of you. This is Trebonius.

Yes, you know everyone. All of the men think very highly of you. This is Trebonius.

Brutus

He is welcome hither.

He is welcome here.

Cassius

This Decius Brutus.

This is Decius Brutus.

Brutus

He is welcome too.

He is also welcome.

Cassius

This, Casca; this, Cinna; and this, Metellus Cimber.

This is Casca, Cinna, and Metellus Cimber.

Brutus

They are all welcome.-- What watchful cares do interpose themselves Betwixt your eyes and night?

They are all welcome. What brings you here this time of night?

Cassius

Shall I entreat a word?

I was hoping to have a word with you.

Brutus and Cassius whisper.

Decius Brutus

Here lies the east: doth not the day break here?

This is the east. Doesn't the sun rise here?

Casca

No.

No.

Cinna

O, pardon, sir, it doth, and yon grey lines That fret the clouds are messengers of day.

Pardon me, sir, it is. The gray line over there is the rising of the sun.

Casca

You shall confess that you are both deceived. Here, as I point my sword, the Sun arises; Which is a great way growing on the South, Weighing the youthful season of the year. Some two months hence, up higher toward the North He first presents his fire; and the high East Stands, as the Capitol, directly here.

I think you are both wrong. See where I'm pointing my sword. The sun is rising in the south because of the time of year. In two months, it will rise higher in the north. The capitol is over there.

Brutus

Give me your hands all over, one by one.

Give me your hands, one over the other.

Cassius

And let us swear our resolution.

Let's swear an oath.

Brutus

No, not an oath: if not the face of men, The sufferance of our souls, the time's abuse-- If these be motives weak, break off betimes, And every man hence to his idle bed; So let high-sighted tyranny range on, Till each man drop by lottery. But if these, As I am sure they do, bear fire enough To kindle cowards, and to steel with valour The melting spirits of women; then, countrymen, What need we any spur but our own cause To prick us to redress? what other bond Than secret Romans, that have spoke the word, And will not palter? and what other oath Than honesty to honesty engaged, That this shall be, or we will fall for it? Swear priests, and cowards, and men cautelous, Old feeble carrions, and such suffering souls That welcome wrongs; unto bad causes swear Such creatures as men doubt: but do not stain The even virtue of our enterprise, Nor th' insuppressive mettle of our spirits, To think that or our cause or our performance Did need an oath; when every drop of blood That every Roman bears, and nobly bears, Is guilty of a several bastardy, If he do break the smallest particle Of any promise that hath pass'd from him.

No, not an oath. We don't need to swear an oath to one another. Oaths are for cowards or old men. We have enough motivation to spur us to action. Our word is good enough.

Cassius

But what of Cicero? Shall we sound him? I think he will stand very strong with us.

What about Cicero? Should we get him? I think he will support us.

Casca

Let us not leave him out.

Let's not leave him out.

Cinna

No, by no means.

No, by no means.

Metellus Cimber

O, let us have him! for his silver hairs Will purchase us a good opinion, And buy men's voices to commend our deeds: It shall be said, his judgment ruled our hands; Our youths and wildness shall no whit appear, But all be buried in his gravity.

Oh, let's include him. His age and wisdom will make us appear noteworthy and make men listen to us. He will also take the blame for our actions, since we are young.

Brutus

O, name him not! let us not break with him; For he will never follow any thing That other men begin.

I don't think we should include him. He'll never go along with anything like this.

Cassius

Then leave him out.

Then leave him out.

Casca

Indeed, he is not fit.

I don't think he is right.

Decius Brutus

Shall no man else be touch'd but only Caesar?

Are we only going after Caesar?

Cassius

Decius, well urged.--I think it is not meet, Mark Antony, so well beloved of Caesar, Should outlive Caesar: we shall find of him A shrewd contriver; and you know his means, If he improve them, may well stretch so far As to annoy us all: which to prevent, Let Antony and Caesar fall together.

Good question, Decius. I think Mark Antony may give us some trouble. So, if he does, let him fall with Caesar.

Brutus

Our course will seem too bloody, Caius Cassius, To cut the head off, and then hack the limbs, Like wrath in death, and envy afterwards; For Antony is but a limb of Caesar. Let us be sacrificers, but not butchers, Caius. We all stand up against the spirit of Caesar; And in the spirit of men there is no blood: O, that we then could come by Caesar's spirit, And not dismember Caesar! But, alas, Caesar must bleed for it! And, gentle friends, Let's kill him boldly, but not wrathfully; Let's carve him as a dish fit for the gods, Not hew him as a carcass fit for hounds; And let our hearts, as subtle masters do, Stir up their servants to an act of rage, And after seem to chide 'em. This shall mark Our purpose necessary, and not envious; Which so appearing to the common eyes, We shall be call'd purgers, not murderers. And for Mark Antony, think not of him; For he can do no more than Caesar's arm When Caesar's head is off.

I don't think that will be necessary, Cassius. Antony just follows Caesar. With Caesar gone, Antony will be no trouble. We must go about this properly and not make Caesar seem like a martyr. We do not want to be seen as murderers, but purgers of evil.

Cassius

Yet I do fear him; For in th' ingrafted love he bears to Caesar--

I still fear him, because of his devotion to Caesar.

Brutus

Alas, good Cassius, do not think of him: If he love Caesar, all that he can do Is to himself,--take thought and die for Caesar. And that were much he should; for he is given To sports, to wildness, and much company.

Don't think of him, Cassius. If he loves Caesar, all he can do is die for him. He probably will die anyway the way he lives.

Trebonius

There is no fear in him; let him not die; For he will live, and laugh at this hereafter.

No one should fear him. Don't kill him. He'll probably live and laugh about this later.

Clock strikes.

Brutus

Peace! count the clock.

Be quiet! What time is it?

Cassius

The clock hath stricken three.

Three o'clock.

Trebonius

'Tis time to part.

It's time to go.

Cassius

But it is doubtful yet Whether Caesar will come forth today or no; For he is superstitious grown of late, Quite from the main opinion he held once Of fantasy, of dreams, and ceremonies. It may be these apparent prodigies, The unaccustom'd terror of this night, And the persuasion of his augurers May hold him from the Capitol to-day.

We still don't know if Caesar will show in the Capitol today. He has been very superstitious lately.

Decius Brutus

Never fear that: if he be so resolved, I can o'ersway him, for he loves to hear That unicorns may be betray'd with trees, And bears with glasses, elephants with holes, Lions with toils, and men with flatterers: But when I tell him he hates flatterers, He says he does, being then most flattered. Let me work; For I can give his humor the true bent, And I will bring him to the Capitol.

Don't worry. I can get him to the Capitol. He loves to hear flattery, so I will get him there by flattering him.

Cassius

Nay, we will all of us be there to fetch him.

No, we will all go to get him.

Brutus

By the eighth hour: is that the uttermost?

By eight o'clock. Is that the time?

Cinna

Be that the uttermost; and fail not then.

I think so.

Metellus Cimber

Caius Ligarius doth bear Caesar hard, Who rated him for speaking well of Pompey: I wonder none of you have thought of him.

Caius Ligarius has reason to hate Caesar for berating him when he spoke well of Pompey. Have any of you thought about him?

Brutus

Now, good Metellus, go along by him: He loves me well, and I have given him reason; Send him but hither, and I'll fashion him.

Good, Metellus. Go get him. He loves me, as well he should. Send him here and I'll convince him.

Cassius

The morning comes upon 's. We'll leave you, Brutus;-- And, friends, disperse yourselves, but all remember What you have said, and show yourselves true Romans.

The morning is here. We'll leave you, Brutus. Friends, let's go our separate ways, but remember what you have said here, and show yourselves as true Romans.

Brutus

Good gentlemen, look fresh and merrily; Let not our looks put on our purposes, But bear it as our Roman actors do, With untired spirits and formal constancy: And so, good morrow to you every one.--

Good gentlemen, you must look fresh and happy. You cannot let on our purpose with your appearances. Let's be like Roman actors, tireless spirits and well-composed faces.

Exit all but Brutus.

Boy! Lucius!--Fast asleep? It is no matter; Enjoy the honey-heavy dew of slumber: Thou hast no figures nor no fantasies, Which busy care draws in the brains of men; Therefore thou sleep'st so sound.

Boy! Lucius! Are you asleep? No matter. Enjoy the heavenly state of sleep. You have nothing to keep you from sleeping soundly.

Enter Portia

Portia

Brutus, my lord!

Brutus, my lord!

Brutus

Portia, what mean you? wherefore rise you now? It is not for your health thus to commit Your weak condition to the raw-cold morning.

Portia, what are you doing up? It's not healthy for you to be up in the cold morning air in your weak condition.

Portia

Nor for yours neither. You've ungently, Brutus, Stole from my bed: and yesternight, at supper, You suddenly arose, and walk'd about, Musing and sighing, with your arms across; And, when I ask'd you what the matter was, You stared upon me with ungentle looks: I urged you further; then you scratch'd your head, And too impatiently stamp'd with your foot: Yet I insisted, yet you answer'd not; But, with an angry wafture of your hand, Gave sign for me to leave you. So I did; Fearing to strengthen that impatience Which seem'd too much enkindled; and withal Hoping it was but an effect of humour, Which sometime hath his hour with every man. It will not let you eat, nor talk, nor sleep; And, could it work so much upon your shape As it hath much prevail'd on your condition, I should not know you, Brutus. Dear my lord, Make me acquainted with your cause of grief.

It's not good for you, either. You urgently go up from bed, Brutus, and yesterday, at dinner, you suddenly got up and walked around thinking and sighing with your arms crossed. When I asked you what the matter was, you stared at me angrily. You stomped your foot when I inquired more. Then, you refused to answer me and waved me off. I don't know what is wrong with you, but you can't eat, or talk, or sleep. You're just not yourself, Brutus. Please, tell me what's wrong with you.

Brutus

I am not well in health, and that is all.

I just haven't been feeling well, lately.

Portia

Brutus is wise, and, were he not in health, He would embrace the means to come by it.

You are a smart man, and if your health were compromised, you would seek treatment.

Brutus

Why, so I do. Good Portia, go to bed.

I am. Now, go to bed, dear Portia.

Portia

Is Brutus sick? and is it physical To walk unbraced and suck up the humours Of the dank morning? What, is Brutus sick, And will he steal out of his wholesome bed To dare the vile contagion of the night, And tempt the rheumy and unpurged air To add unto his sickness? No, my Brutus; You have some sick offense within your mind, Which, by the right and virtue of my place, I ought to know of: and, upon my knees, I charge you, by my once commended beauty, By all your vows of love, and that great vow Which did incorporate and make us one, That you unfold to me, yourself, your half, Why you are heavy, and what men to-night Have had resort to you; for here have been Some six or seven, who did hide their faces Even from darkness.

Are you sick? It can't be something physical, if you're walking around in the damp morning. And, what makes you get out of bed to dare the germs that are in the night air. No, Brutus, you are not sick, unless it is in your mind. You are my husband, so I know. Now, tell me why you are so heavy-hearted. Who were the men you talking to? I saw six or seven here in the dark.

Brutus

Kneel not, gentle Portia.

Don't ask, Portia.

Portia

I should not need, if you were gentle Brutus. Within the bond of marriage, tell me, Brutus, Is it excepted I should know no secrets That appertain to you? Am I yourself But, as it were, in sort or limitation,-- To keep with you at meals, comfort your bed, And talk to you sometimes? Dwell I but in the suburbs Of your good pleasure? If it be no more, Portia is Brutus' harlot, not his wife.

I wouldn't have to if you were honest to your marriage vows. Tell me, Brutus. Am I not to know everything about my husband? Am I just supposed to spend time with you at meals and at bedtime? If so, I'm not your wife, I'm your whore.

Brutus

You are my true and honorable wife; As dear to me as are the ruddy drops That visit my sad heart.

You are my wonderful and honorable wife. You are so dear to me.

Portia

If this were true, then should I know this secret. I grant I am a woman; but withal A woman that Lord Brutus took to wife: I grant I am a woman; but withal A woman well reputed, Cato's daughter. Think you I am no stronger than my sex, Being so father'd and so husbanded? Tell me your counsels, I will not disclose 'em. I have made strong proof of my constancy, Giving myself a voluntary wound Here in the thigh: can I bear that with patience And not my husband's secrets?

If this is true, then I should know this secret. Granted, I am just a woman, but I am the woman you chose to be your wife. I am the daughter of Cato, but you don't think I am very strong. Tell me your secret and I will not tell a soul. I have proven my faithfulness, by giving myself a wound in my thigh. If I can bear that pain, then I can bear my husband's secrets.

Brutus

O ye gods, Render me worthy of this noble wife!

Oh, gods, make me worthy of this noble wife.

Knocking within.

Hark, hark, one knocks: Portia, go in awhile; And by and by thy bosom shall partake The secrets of my heart: All my engagements I will construe to thee, All the charactery of my sad brows. Leave me with haste.

Hello! Someone is knocking, Portia. Please go in awhile, and I will come in and tell you what's going on. Hurry and leave.

Exit Portia.

--Lucius, who's that knocks?

Lucius, who's knocking?

Re-enter Lucius with Ligarius.

Lucius

Here is a sick man that would speak with you.

A sick man is here and he wants to speak with you.

Brutus

Caius Ligarius, that Metellus spake of.-- Boy, stand aside.--Caius Ligarius,--how?

Caius Ligarius, you are the one Metellus spoke of. Lucius, go away. How are you, Ligarius?

Ligarius

Vouchsafe good-morrow from a feeble tongue.

Good morning. I am not feeling well.

Brutus

O, what a time have you chose out, brave Caius, To wear a kerchief! Would you were not sick!

What a time to be sick, brave Caius. You should cover your head and you would not be sick!

Ligarius

I am not sick, if Brutus have in hand Any exploit worthy the name of honour.

I am not sick, if you have something worthy for me to do.

Brutus

Such an exploit have I in hand, Ligarius, Had you a healthful ear to hear of it.

I do, if you are healthy enough to hear it.

Ligarius

By all the gods that Romans bow before, I here discard my sickness. Soul of Rome! Brave son, derived from honorable loins! Thou, like an exorcist, hast conjured up My mortified spirit. Now bid me run, And I will strive with things impossible; Yea, get the better of them. What's to do?

I swear by all the gods, I am no longer sick. You have made me well. Now, tell me what you want me to do.

Brutus

A piece of work that will make sick men whole.

What I am going to tell you may make sick men whole.

Ligarius

But are not some whole that we must make sick?

Will is making some healthy men sick?

Brutus

That must we also. What it is, my Caius, I shall unfold to thee, as we are going, To whom it must be done.

It may, also. I will tell you as we go to whom it must be done.

Ligarius

Set on your foot; And with a heart new-fired I follow you, To do I know not what: but it sufficeth That Brutus leads me on.

I'm following you, although I still don't know why. But as long as you're leading, I'm following.

Brutus

Follow me then.

Come this way, then.

Exit.

Scene II: Caesar's house.

Thunder and lightning. Enter Caesar, in his night-gown.

Caesar

Nor heaven nor earth have been at peace tonight: Thrice hath Calpurnia in her sleep cried out, "Help, ho! They murder Caesar!"--Who's within?

Neither heaven nor earth is at peace this night. Three times Calpurnia has cried out in her sleep, "Help! They murder Caesar!" Who's there?

Servant

My lord?

Your servant, my lord?

Caesar

? Go bid the priests do present sacrifice, And bring me their opinions of success.

Tell the priests to present a sacrifice and come tell me what they think.

Servant

I will, my lord.

I will, my lord.

Exit.

Enter Calpurnia.

Calpurnia

What mean you, Caesar? Think you to walk forth? You shall not stir out of your house to-day.

What's going on, Caesar? Do you mean to go out today? You shouldn't.

Caesar

Caesar shall forth: the things that threaten me Ne'er look but on my back; when they shall see The face of Caesar, they are vanished.

I am going out because those that wish to cause me harm always talk behind my back. When I appear, they vanish.

Calpurnia

Caesar, I never stood on ceremonies, Yet now they fright me. There is one within, Besides the things that we have heard and seen, Recounts most horrid sights seen by the watch. A lioness hath whelped in the streets; And graves have yawn'd, and yielded up their dead; Fierce fiery warriors fight upon the clouds, In ranks and squadrons and right form of war, Which drizzled blood upon the Capitol; The noise of battle hurtled in the air, Horses did neigh, and dying men did groan; And ghosts did shriek and squeal about the streets. O Caesar,these things are beyond all use, And I do fear them!

Caesar, I have never been superstitious, but now I am frightened. A lioness was seen in the streets, graves have opened revealing the dead, fire has been set throughout the Capitol, and the noise of battle heard in the air with the cries of horses, dying men, and shrieking ghosts. Oh, Caesar! There is no explanation for these occurrences, and I am afraid.

Caesar

What can be avoided Whose end is purposed by the mighty gods? Yet Caesar shall go forth; for these predictions Are to the world in general as to Caesar.

Who can avoid what the gods ordain? So, I shall go out and face these predictions for myself and for Rome.

Calpurnia

When beggars die, there are no comets seen; The heavens themselves blaze forth the death of princes.

When beggars die, nothing extraordinary happens, but when a prince dies, strange things are seen.

Caesar

Cowards die many times before their deaths; The valiant never taste of death but once. Of all the wonders that I yet have heard, It seems to me most strange that men should fear; Seeing that death, a necessary end, Will come when it will come.--

Cowards die many deaths, but a courageous man only experiences death once. Death is inevitable, so I don't understand why men fear it.

Re-enter Servant.

What say the augurers?

What did the priests say?

Servant

They would not have you to stir forth to-day. Plucking the entrails of an offering forth, They could not find a heart within the beast.

They don't think you should come out today. When they performed the sacrifice, they couldn't find the heart.

Caesar

The gods do this in shame of cowardice: Caesar should be a beast without a heart, If he should stay at home today for fear. No, Caesar shall not: danger knows full well That Caesar is more dangerous than he: We are two lions litter'd in one day, And I the elder and more terrible; And Caesar shall go forth.

It is a sign from the gods, that a beast without a heart is a coward. I will not stay home today in fear. I, myself, am dangerous. So, I will go.

Calpurnia

Alas, my lord, Your wisdom is consumed in confidence! Do not go forth to-day: call it my fear That keeps you in the house, and not your own. We'll send Mark Antony to the Senate-house, And he shall say you are not well to-day: Let me, upon my knee, prevail in this.

Please, my lord, don't go. Blame it on my fear. Let Mark Antony go instead, and say that you are ill. I am begging you. Do not go.

Caesar

Mark Antony shall say I am not well, And, for thy humor, I will stay at home.

Mark Antony can say I am not well, and I will stay home for you.

Enter Decius Brutus

Here's Decius Brutus, he shall tell them so.

Here's Decius Brutus. He can tell them.

Decius Brutus

Caesar, all hail! Good morrow, worthy Caesar: I come to fetch you to the Senate-house.

All hail, Caesar! Good morning, sir. I have come to escort you to the senate-house.

Caesar

And you are come in very happy time To bear my greeting to the Senators, And tell them that I will not come to-day. Cannot, is false; and that I dare not, falser: I will not come to-day. Tell them so, Decius.

I am glad you are here. You can tell the senators that I will not be coming today, well cannot is not really true, nor is I dare not. Just tell them I'm not coming.

Calpurnia

Say he is sick.

Say he is sick.

Caesar

Shall Caesar send a lie? Have I in conquest stretch'd mine arm so far, To be afeard to tell grey-beards the truth?-- Decius, go tell them Caesar will not come.

Shall I tell a lie? Am I afraid to tell the old men the truth? Decius, go tell I am not coming.

Decius Brutus

Most mighty Caesar, let me know some cause, Lest I be laugh'd at when I tell them so.

You must give me a reason, so I will not be laughed at.

Caesar

The cause is in my will; I will not come: That is enough to satisfy the Senate. But, for your private satisfaction, Because I love you, I will let you know: Calpurnia here, my wife, stays me at home: She dreamt to-night she saw my statua, Which, like a fountain with an hundred spouts, Did run pure blood; and many lusty Romans Came smiling and did bathe their hands in it: And these does she apply for warnings and portents And evils imminent; and on her knee Hath begg'd that I will stay at home to-day.

Just tell them I don't want to come. That should be enough. But, since I love you, I will tell you in private, Calpurnia had a dream and saw me murdered. She has begged me to stay home today.

Decius Brutus

This dream is all amiss interpreted: It was a vision fair and fortunate. Your statue spouting blood in many pipes, In which so many smiling Romans bathed, Signifies that from you great Rome shall suck Reviving blood; and that great men shall press For tinctures, stains, relics, and cognizance. This by Calpurnia's dream is signified.

The dream is misinterpreted. It was not the blood of your death but the blood of birth. Rome is going to experience a revival under you. This is what Calpurnia's dream meant.

Caesar

And this way have you well expounded it.

That is a good explanation.

Decius Brutus

I have, when you have heard what I can say; And know it now: The Senate have concluded To give this day a crown to mighty Caesar. If you shall send them word you will not come, Their minds may change. Besides, it were a mock Apt to be render'd, for someone to say "Break up the Senate till another time, When Caesar's wife shall meet with better dreams." If Caesar hide himself, shall they not whisper "Lo, Caesar is afraid"? Pardon me, Caesar; for my dear dear love To your proceeding bids me tell you this; And reason to my love is liable.

I know because today the senate decided to give you a crown. If you don't come, they may change their minds. Some may even question your abilities if you listen to your wife's dreams. Pardon my frankness, I tell you this out of my love for you.

Caesar

How foolish do your fears seem now, Calpurnia! I am ashamed I did yield to them. Give me my robe, for I will go.

See, Calpurnia, how foolish fear is. I ashamed I listened to them. Give me my robe, and I will go.

Enter Publius, Brutus, Ligarius, Metellus, Casca, Trebonius, and Cinna.

And look where Publius is come to fetch me.

Now, Publius has come to get me.

Publius

Good morrow, Caesar.

Good morning, Caesar.

Caesar

Welcome, Publius.-- What, Brutus, are you stirr'd so early too?-- Good morrow, Casca.--Caius Ligarius, Caesar was ne'er so much your enemy As that same ague which hath made you lean.-- What is't o'clock?

Welcome, Publius. What are you doing up so early, Brutus? Good morning, Casca. Caius Ligarius, you are looking sickly. What time is it?

Brutus

Caesar, 'tis strucken eight.

Caesar, it's eight o'clock.

Caesar

I thank you for your pains and courtesy.

Thank you.

Enter Antony.

See! Antony, that revels long o'nights, Is notwithstanding up.--Good morrow, Antony.

Even the partier, Antony, is up. Good morning, Antony!

Antony

So to most noble Caesar.

Same to you, most noble Caesar.

Caesar

Bid them prepare within: I am to blame to be thus waited for.-- Now, Cinna;--now, Metellus;--what, Trebonius! I have an hour's talk in store for you: Remember that you call on me to-day; Be near me, that I may remember you.

Tell them to get ready and that I am to blame for keeping them waiting. Cinna, Mettellus, and Trebonius, I have a long talk prepared for you, so stay close by.

Trebonius

Caesar, I will. [Aside.] and so near will I be, That your best friends shall wish I had been further.

I will, Caesar.

Aside.

I will be so close that your best friends will wish I had been further away.

Caesar

Good friends, go in, and taste some wine with me; And we, like friends, will straightway go together.

My good friends, let's go in and drink some wine and then, we will go together.

Brutus

[Aside.] That every like is not the same, O Caesar, The heart of Brutus yearns to think upon!

Aside.

I wish things could be the same, Caesar. I hate to think of the future.

Exit all.

Scene III: A street near the Capitol.

Enter Artemidorus, reading a paper.

Artemidorus

"Caesar, beware of Brutus; take heed of Cassius; come not near Casca; have an eye to Cinna; trust not Trebonius; mark well Metellus Cimber; Decius Brutus loves thee not; thou hast wrong'd Caius Ligarius. There is but one mind in all these men, and it is bent against Caesar. If thou be'st not immortal, look about you: security gives way to conspiracy. The mighty gods defend thee! Thy lover, Artemidorus." Here will I stand till Caesar pass along, And as a suitor will I give him this. My heart laments that virtue cannot live Out of the teeth of emulation.-- If thou read this, O Caesar, thou mayest live; If not, the Fates with traitors do contrive.

"Caesar, beware of Brutus and take heed of Cassius. Do not go near Casca, and keep an eye on Cinna. Don't trust Trebonius or Metellus Cimber. Decius Brutus doesn't love you, and you have the wrong idea about Caius Ligarius. These men are of one mind and it is anti-Caesar. If you are not immortal, look around and recognize the conspiracy. May the mighty gods defend you. Your friend, Artemidorus." I will stand here until Caesar passes by and give him this. My heart aches that a good man cannot be without enemies. If Caesar reads this, he may live. If not, then Fate conspires with traitors.

Exit.

Scene IV: Another part of the same street, before the house of Brutus.

Enter Portia and Lucius.

Portia

I pr'ythee, boy, run to the Senate-house; Stay not to answer me, but get thee gone. Why dost thou stay?

Please, boy, run to the senate-house. Get going. Why are you still here?

Lucius

To know my errand, madam.

I need to know why I'm going, madam.

Portia

I would have had thee there, and here again, Ere I can tell thee what thou shouldst do there.-- [Aside.] O constancy, be strong upon my side! Set a huge mountain 'tween my heart and tongue! I have a man's mind, but a woman's might. How hard it is for women to keep counsel!-- Art thou here yet?

You could have been there and back again by the time I can tell you what you are to do there. Oh Lord, help me be strong. Keep my heart from controlling my mouth. It is so hard for a woman to keep a secret. Are you still here?

Lucius

Madam, what should I do? Run to the Capitol, and nothing else? And so return to you, and nothing else?

Madam, what do you want me to do? Just go there and back, nothing else?

Portia

Yes, bring me word, boy, if thy lord look well, For he went sickly forth: and take good note What Caesar doth, what suitors press to him. Hark, boy! what noise is that?

Yes, bring me word, boy, if your lord looked okay. He was sick when he went. Also, take a look at Caesar, and see what men are near him. Listen, boy! What was that noise?

Lucius

I hear none, madam.

I didn't hear anything.

Portia

Pr'ythee, listen well: I heard a bustling rumour, like a fray, And the wind brings it from the Capitol.

Please listen harder. I heard a bustling noise from the direction of the Capitol.

Enter the Soothsayer.

Portia

Come hither, fellow: Which way hast thou been?

Come here, fellow. Where are you coming from?

Soothsayer

At mine own house, good lady.

From my house, good lady.

Portia

What is't o'clock?

What time is it?

Soothsayer

About the ninth hour, lady.

It's about nine o'clock.

Portia

Is Caesar yet gone to the Capitol?

Has Caesar gone to the Capitol, yet?

Soothsayer

Madam, not yet: I go to take my stand To see him pass on to the Capitol.

Not yet, madam. I haven't seen him pass by.

Portia

Thou hast some suit to Caesar, hast thou not?

You work for Caesar, right?

Soothsayer

That I have, lady: if it will please Caesar To be so good to Caesar as to hear me, I shall beseech him to befriend himself.

Yes. When it pleases him to hear me out, I am a friend to him.

Portia

Why, know'st thou any harm's intended towards him?

Do you know of any harm intended towards him?

Soothsayer

None that I know will be, much that I fear may chance. Good morrow to you.--Here the street is narrow: The throng that follows Caesar at the heels, Of Senators, of Praetors, common suitors, Will crowd a feeble man almost to death: I'll get me to a place more void, and there Speak to great Caesar as he comes along.

None that I know of, although I fear there may be a chance. Good day to you. I need to get going before Caesar and his followers come through this narrow street and trample me to death. I need to get to a better place so I may speak to Caesar.

Exit.

Portia

I must go in.--[Aside.] Ah me, how weak a thing The heart of woman is!--O Brutus, The heavens speed thee in thine enterprise!-- Sure, the boy heard me.--Brutus hath a suit That Caesar will not grant.--O, I grow faint.-- Run, Lucius, and commend me to my lord; Say I am merry: come to me again, And bring me word what he doth say to thee.

I must go inside. Yes, the heart of a woman is weak. Oh Brutus, may the heavens help you in your work. I know the boy heard me. Brutus has a request Caesar will not grant. Oh, I grow weaker. Run, Lucius, and tell my lord I am well and happy. Then, come to me and tell me what he says

Act III

Scene I: Rome. Before the Capitol with the Senate sitting above.

A crowd of people: Artemidorus and the Soothsayer. Flourish. Enter Caesar, Brutus, Cassius, Casca, Decius Brutus, Metellus Cimber, Trebonius, Cinna, Mark Antony, Lepidus, Popilius, Publius, and others.

Caesar

To the Soothsayer.

The Ides of March are come.

The ides of March have come.

Soothsayer

Ay, Caesar; but not gone.

Yes, but they are not gone.

Artemidorus

Hail, Caesar! read this schedule.

Hail, Caesar! Read this schedule.

Decius Brutus

Trebonius doth desire you to o'er-read, At your best leisure, this his humble suit.

Trebonius needs you to read over this petition, when you get a moment.

Artemidorus

O Caesar, read mine first; for mine's a suit That touches Caesar nearer: read it, great Caesar.

Oh Caesar, read mine first. My petition is more personal. Read it, great Caesar.

Caesar

What touches us ourself shall be last served.

If it has something to do with me, I'll read it last.

Artemidorus

Delay not, Caesar; read it instantly.

Don't delay, Caesar. Read it, now.

Caesar

What, is the fellow mad?

Have you gone crazy?

Publius

Sirrah, give place.

Stand back, sir.

Cassius

What, urge you your petitions in the street? Come to the Capitol.

Are you petitioning in the streets? Come to the Capitol.

Caesar goes up to the Senate-House and the rest follows.

Popilius

I wish your enterprise to-day may thrive.

I hope your work goes well today.

Cassius

What enterprise, Popilius?

What work, Popilius?

Popilius

Fare you well. Advances to Caesar.

Goodbye then.

Advances towards Caesar.

Brutus

What said Popilius Lena?

What did Popilius Lena say?

Cassius

He wish'd to-day our enterprise might thrive. I fear our purpose is discovered.

He hoped our work would go well today. I'm afraid he knows what we're planning.

Brutus

Look, how he makes to Caesar: mark him.

Look how he is getting closer to Caesar. Watch him.

Cassius

Casca, be sudden, for we fear prevention.-- Brutus, what shall be done? If this be known, Cassius or Caesar never shall turn back, For I will slay myself.

Casca, act quickly. We don't want to be prevented. Brutus, what should we do? If we are discovered, I will kill myself.

Brutus

Cassius, be constant: Popilius Lena speaks not of our purposes; For, look, he smiles, and Caesar doth not change.

Be calm, Cassius. Popilius Lena is not talking about our plan. Look at him smiling, and Caesar's expression has not changed.

Cassius

Trebonius knows his time, for, look you, Brutus, He draws Mark Antony out of the way.

Trebonius knows what to do. He is drawing Mark Antony away.

Exit Antony and Trebonius.

Decius Brutus

Where is Metellus Cimber? Let him go, And presently prefer his suit to Caesar.

Where is Metellus Cimber? Let him go and present his case to Caesar.

Brutus

He is address'd; press near and second him.

He is presenting. Go closer and help him.

Cinna

Casca, you are the first that rears your hand.

Casca, you are the first to strike.

Caesar

What is now amiss That Caesar and his Senate must redress?

Are we all ready? What do the senate and I need to address?

Metellus Cimber

Most high, most mighty, and most puissant Caesar, Metellus Cimber throws before thy seat An humble heart.

Most high and mighty Caesar, I throw myself at your feet with a humble heart...

Kneeling.

Caesar

I must prevent thee, Cimber. These couchings and these lowly courtesies Might fire the blood of ordinary men, And turn pre-ordinance and first decree Into the law of children. Be not fond, To think that Caesar bears such rebel blood That will be thaw'd from the true quality With that which melteth fools; I mean, sweet words, Low-crooked curtsies, and base spaniel-fawning. Thy brother by decree is banished: If thou dost bend, and pray, and fawn for him, I spurn thee like a cur out of my way.

No need, Cimber. Your actions may make men think that I'm persuaded by such flattery. Your brother has been banished, and I will not grant him a pardon without a good reason

Metellus Cimber

Caesar, thou dost me wrong.

Isn't my voice enough to petition for my brother's pardon?

METELLUS

Caesar, thou dost me wrong.

CAESAR

Caesar did never wrong but with just cause, Nor without cause will he be satisfied.

METELLUS

Is there no voice more worthy than my own, To sound more sweetly in great Caesar's ear For the repealing of my banish'd brother?

Brutus

I kiss thy hand, but not in flattery, Caesar; Desiring thee that Publius Cimber may Have an immediate freedom of repeal.

I kiss your hand, not out of flattery, but to show my desire that you grant Publius Cimber's claim to freedom.

Caesar

What, Brutus?

What, Brutus!

Cassius

Pardon, Caesar; Caesar, pardon: As low as to thy foot doth Cassius fall, To beg enfranchisement for Publius Cimber.

Pardon me, Caesar. I bow at your feet to plea for Publius Cimber.

Caesar

I could be well moved, if I were as you; If I could pray to move, prayers would move me: But I am constant as the northern star, Of whose true-fix'd and resting quality There is no fellow in the firmament. The skies are painted with unnumber'd sparks, They are all fire, and every one doth shine; But there's but one in all doth hold his place: So in the world; 'tis furnish'd well with men, And men are flesh and blood, and apprehensive; Yet in the number I do know but one That unassailable holds on his rank, Unshaked of motion: and that I am he, Let me a little show it, even in this,-- That I was constant Cimber should be banish'd, And constant do remain to keep him so.

I could be convinced if, I were you. But I am as immovable as the North Star. They are all made of fire, but only one remains unmoving. It is the same with men. I am the only one who will not be moved. I remain firm in my decision.

Cinna

O Caesar,--

Oh, Caesar...

Caesar

Hence! wilt thou lift up Olympus?

What do you want me to do? Lift up Mount Olympus?

Decius Brutus

Great Caesar,--

Great Caesar...

Caesar

Doth not Brutus bootless kneel?

Didn't Brutus beg for him?

Casca

Speak, hands, for me!

Hands, speak for me!

Casca first, then the other Conspirators and Brutus stab Caesar.

Caesar

Et tu, Brute?-- Then fall, Caesar!

And you, Brute! Then, die Caesar!

Dies.

Cinna

Liberty! Freedom! Tyranny is dead!-- Run hence, proclaim, cry it about the streets.

Liberty! Freedom! Tyranny is dead! Run and proclaim it in the streets.

Cassius

Some to the common pulpits and cry out, "Liberty, freedom, and enfranchisement!"

Go to the commons and cry out, "Liberty, freedom, and democracy!"

Brutus

People and Senators, be not affrighted; Fly not; stand still; ambition's debt is paid.

Don't be afraid, people and senators. Don't run off. Stay because Caesar was killed by his ambition.

Casca

Go to the pulpit, Brutus.

Go to the pulpit, Brutus.

Decius Brutus

And Cassius too.

And Cassius, too.

Brutus

Where's Publius?

Where's Publius?

Cinna

Here, quite confounded with this mutiny.

He's here and quite confused with the mutiny.

Metellus Cimber

Stand fast together, lest some friend of Caesar's Should chance--

Stand by each other, or else some friend of Caesar's may...

Brutus

Talk not of standing.--Publius, good cheer! There is no harm intended to your person, Nor to no Roman else: so tell them, Publius.

Don't talk like that. Publius, be happy. No harm is meant for you or any other Roman. Tell them Publius.

Cassius

And leave us, Publius; lest that the people Rushing on us, should do your age some mischief.

Leave us, Publius, in case the people coming towards us should harm you.

Brutus

Do so;--and let no man abide this deed But we the doers.

Go ahead. No one will claim this deed except those who did it.

Re-enter Trebonius.

Cassius

Where's Antony?

Where is Antony?

Trebonius

Fled to his house amazed. Men, wives, and children stare, cry out, and run, As it were doomsday.

He ran to his house, awestruck. Men, wives, and children cry out and run like it is the end of the world.

Brutus

Fates, we will know your pleasures: That we shall die, we know; 'tis but the time And drawing days out, that men stand upon.

We will soon know what Fate has in store for us. We will all die someday, although, we will try to postpone it.

Cassius

Why, he that cuts off twenty years of life Cuts off so many years of fearing death.

If one cuts off twenty years from his life, that's twenty years he doesn't fear death.

Brutus

Grant that, and then is death a benefit: So are we Caesar's friends, that have abridged His time of fearing death.-- Stoop, Romans, stoop, And let us bathe our hands in Caesar's blood Up to the elbows, and besmear our swords: Then walk we forth, even to the market-place, And waving our red weapons o'er our heads, Let's all cry, "Peace, freedom, and liberty!"

That's true, so we are Caesar's friends because we have shortened his life of fearing death. Bend, gentlemen, and soak your hands in Caesar's blood up to the elbow. Smear the blood on your sword, and let's walk to the market-place and cry, "Peace, freedom, and liberty."

Cassius

Stoop then, and wash. How many ages hence Shall this our lofty scene be acted o'er In States unborn and accents yet unknown!

Bend and wash yourselves in Caesar's blood. How many times will our scene be repeated around the world!

Brutus

How many times shall Caesar bleed in sport, That now on Pompey's basis lies along No worthier than the dust!

How many times will this be replayed even though Caesar now lies in the dirt!

Cassius

So oft as that shall be, So often shall the knot of us be call'd The men that gave their country liberty

However many times, we will be the men who freed their fellow countrymen.

Decius Brutus

What, shall we forth?

Shall we go?

Cassius

Ay, every man away: Brutus shall lead; and we will grace his heels With the most boldest and best hearts of Rome.

Yes, let's go everyone. Brutus leads and we will follow him, the boldest men in all of Rome.

Enter a servant.

Brutus

Soft, who comes here?

Shh! Who is this? A friend of Antony's.

Servant

Thus, Brutus, did my master bid me kneel; Thus did Mark Antony bid me fall down; And, being prostrate, thus he bade me say: Brutus is noble, wise, valiant, and honest; Caesar was mighty, bold, royal, and loving; Say I love Brutus and I honor him; Say I fear'd Caesar, honour'd him, and loved him. If Brutus will vouchsafe that Antony May safely come to him, and be resolved How Caesar hath deserved to lie in death, Mark Antony shall not love Caesar dead So well as Brutus living; but will follow The fortunes and affairs of noble Brutus Thorough the hazards of this untrod state With all true faith. So says my master Antony.

Brutus, my master told me to kneel. Mark Antony told me to fall down and say, "Brutus is noble wise, valiant, and honest. Caesar was mighty, bold, royal, and loving. I love Brutus and I honor him. I was afraid of Caesar, but I honored and loved him. If Brutus can promise his safety, Antony will come to him and listen to how Caesar came to deserve to die. Mark Antony will not love Caesar, dead, more than the living Brutus. He will follow Brutus and be faithful to him."

Brutus

Thy master is a wise and valiant Roman; I never thought him worse. Tell him, so please him come unto this place, He shall be satisfied and, by my honour, Depart untouch'd.

Your master is a wise and brave Roman. I never thought poorly of him. Tell him to come here and he will not be touched.

Servant

I'll fetch him presently.

I will go get him right now.

Exit.

Brutus

I know that we shall have him well to friend.

It will benefit us to have him as a friend.

Cassius

I wish we may: but yet have I a mind That fears him much; and my misgiving still Falls shrewdly to the purpose.

I hope so, but I am afraid of him.

Brutus

But here comes Antony.--

Here he comes.

Re-enter Antony.

Welcome, Mark Antony.

Welcome, Mark Antony.

Antony

O mighty Caesar! Dost thou lie so low? Are all thy conquests, glories, triumphs, spoils, Shrunk to this little measure? Fare thee well.-- I know not, gentlemen, what you intend, Who else must be let blood, who else is rank: If I myself, there is no hour so fit As Caesar's death-hour, nor no instrument Of half that worth as those your swords, made rich With the most noble blood of all this world. I do beseech ye, if you bear me hard, Now, whilst your purpled hands do reek and smoke, Fulfill your pleasure. Live a thousand years, I shall not find myself so apt to die: No place will please me so, no means of death, As here by Caesar, and by you cut off, The choice and master spirits of this age.

Oh mighty Caesar! You lie so low. All of your triumphs and glories have some to this. Goodbye. I do not know what you gentlemen are thinking, but who else has to die? Me? If so, now's the time. Do it with those swords drenched in noble blood. I beg you, if you have something against me, take care of it now. If I live a thousand years, I will not be more prepared to die as I am right now. No place will please me more, as to die by Caesar.

Brutus

O Antony, beg not your death of us! Though now we must appear bloody and cruel, As, by our hands and this our present act You see we do; yet see you but our hands And this the bleeding business they have done: Our hearts you see not; they are pitiful; And pity to the general wrong of Rome-- As fire drives out fire, so pity pity-- Hath done this deed on Caesar. For your part, To you our swords have leaden points, Mark Antony; Our arms in strength of amity, and our hearts Of brothers' temper, do receive you in With all kind love, good thoughts, and reverence.

Oh, Antony, don't beg us to kill you. I know we must appear bloody and cruel, but you do not know our hearts. They are sad and sad for Rome. You see our swords, Mark Antony, and you see malice, but we receive you with love and acceptance.

Cassius

Your voice shall be as strong as any man's In the disposing of new dignities.

You will be as strong as any man in the development of a new senate.

Brutus

Only be patient till we have appeased The multitude, beside themselves with fear, And then we will deliver you the cause Why I, that did love Caesar when I struck him, Have thus proceeded.

Only be patient while we take care of the people who are beside themselves with fear. Then, we will tell you why we killed Caesar.

Antony

I doubt not of your wisdom. Let each man render me his bloody hand: First, Marcus Brutus, will I shake with you;-- Next, Caius Cassius, do I take your hand;-- Now, Decius Brutus, yours;--now yours, Metellus;-- Yours, Cinna;--and, my valiant Casca, yours;-- Though last, not least in love, yours, good Trebonius. Gentlemen all-- alas, what shall I say? My credit now stands on such slippery ground, That one of two bad ways you must conceit me, Either a coward or a flatterer.-- That I did love thee, Caesar, O, 'tis true: If then thy spirit look upon us now, Shall it not grieve thee dearer than thy death To see thy Antony making his peace, Shaking the bloody fingers of thy foes,-- Most noble!--in the presence of thy corse? Had I as many eyes as thou hast wounds, Weeping as fast as they stream forth thy blood, It would become me better than to close In terms of friendship with thine enemies. Pardon me, Julius! Here wast thou bay'd, brave hart; Here didst thou fall; and here thy hunters stand, Sign'd in thy spoil, and crimson'd in thy death.-- O world, thou wast the forest to this hart; And this, indeed, O world, the heart of thee.-- How like a deer strucken by many princes, Dost thou here lie!

I don't doubt your wisdom. Let me shake each of your hands, first, Marcus Brutus and Caius Cassius. Now, Decius Brutus give me your hand and Metellus. Let me shake yours, Cinna and brave Casca. Last but not least, give me your hand Trebonius. What can I say, gentlemen? You must be unsure of how to take me, coward or flatterer. I did love Caesar, and if his spirit is watching us now, I hope he is not grieved by me making peace with his enemies. If I had as many eyes as you have wounds, I would still look better than the act of becoming friends with your murderers. Forgive me, Julius! Here, you were hunted and killed like a deer, stabbed by the swords of many princes!

Cassius

Mark Antony,--

Mark Antony...

Antony

Pardon me, Caius Cassius: The enemies of Caesar shall say this; Then, in a friend, it is cold modesty.

Forgive me, Caius Cassius. Even the enemies of Caesar would say the same thing.

Cassius

I blame you not for praising Caesar so; But what compact mean you to have with us? Will you be prick'd in number of our friends, Or shall we on, and not depend on you?

I don't blame you for praising Caesar, but what is your purpose? Are you our friend or can't we depend on you.

Antony

Therefore I took your hands; but was indeed Sway'd from the point, by looking down on Caesar. Friends am I with you all, and love you all, Upon this hope, that you shall give me reasons Why and wherein Caesar was dangerous.

I took your hands in friendship, but lost my focus when I saw Caesar. I am with you all, and I love you. I hope you can entrust in me your reasons for killing Caesar.

Brutus

Or else were this a savage spectacle: Our reasons are so full of good regard That were you, Antony, the son of Caesar, You should be satisfied.

We had such noble intentions, that even if you were Caesar's son you'd be pleased.

Antony

That's all I seek: And am moreover suitor that I may Produce his body to the market-place; And in the pulpit, as becomes a friend, Speak in the order of his funeral.

That's all I want to know, and I'd like to take his body to the pulpit, like a friend would, and speak at his funeral.

Brutus

You shall, Mark Antony.

You will, Mark Antony.

Cassius

Brutus, a word with you.

Brutus, can I have a word with you.

Aside to Brutus.

You know not what you do; do not consent That Antony speak in his funeral: Know you how much the people may be moved By that which he will utter?

You don't know what you are doing. Don't allow Antony to speak at his funeral. You don't know how the people will be affected by what he will say.

Brutus

By your pardon: I will myself into the pulpit first, And show the reason of our Caesar's death: What Antony shall speak, I will protest He speaks by leave and by permission; And that we are contented Caesar shall Have all true rights and lawful ceremonies. It shall advantage more than do us wrong.

I beg your pardon, but I will speak first and tell everyone why we killed Caesar. I will counter anything Antony will say, but we must allow Caesar to have all the ceremony and rites of someone in his position. It will be to our advantage.

Cassius

I know not what may fall; I like it not.

I don't know what will happen, and I don't like it at all.

Brutus

Mark Antony, here, take you Caesar's body. You shall not in your funeral speech blame us, But speak all good you can devise of Caesar; And say you do't by our permission; Else shall you not have any hand at all About his funeral: and you shall speak In the same pulpit whereto I am going, After my speech is ended.

Mark Antony, take Caesar's body. You may not blame us in your funeral speech. Speak well of Caesar, and let everyone know we've given you permission to speak or else you won't be able to speak at all. You are going to speak after me.

Antony

Be it so; I do desire no more.

That's fine. That's all I want.

Brutus

Prepare the body, then, and follow us.

Prepare the body then, and follow us.

Exit all but Antony.

Antony

O, pardon me, thou bleeding piece of earth, That I am meek and gentle with these butchers! Thou art the ruins of the noblest man That ever lived in the tide of times. Woe to the hand that shed this costly blood! Over thy wounds now do I prophesy,-- Which, like dumb mouths do ope their ruby lips To beg the voice and utterance of my tongue,-- A curse shall light upon the limbs of men; Domestic fury and fierce civil strife Shall cumber all the parts of Italy; Blood and destruction shall be so in use, And dreadful objects so familiar, That mothers shall but smile when they behold Their infants quarter'd with the hands of war; All pity choked with custom of fell deeds: And Caesar's spirit, ranging for revenge, With Ate' by his side come hot from Hell, Shall in these confines with a monarch's voice Cry "Havoc!" and let slip the dogs of war, That this foul deed shall smell above the earth With carrion men, groaning for burial.--

Forgive me, Caesar that I am meek and gentle with these butchers! You were the noblest man who ever lived. I curse the hand that shed your blood! Over your wounds I swear a curse upon their lives. Domestic fury and fierce civil strife will erupt all over Italy. It will be so awful and become so customary that mothers will smile when their infants are torn apart. Caesar's spirit will get revenge as it cries in a kingly voice, "Havoc," and the dogs of war are released. Dying men will groan to be buried.

Enter a servant.

You serve Octavius Caesar, do you not?

You are a servant for Octavius Caesar, aren't you?

Servant

I do, Mark Antony.

I am, Mark Antony.

Antony

Caesar did write for him to come to Rome.

Caesar wrote to him and asked him to come to Rome.

Servant

He did receive his letters, and is coming; And bid me say to you by word of mouth,-- [Seeing the body.] O Caesar!--

He did receive his letters and is coming. He asked me to tell you… Oh, Caesar!

Sees the body.

Antony

Thy heart is big, get thee apart and weep. Passion, I see, is catching; for mine eyes, Seeing those beads of sorrow stand in thine, Began to water. Is thy master coming?

Your heart is big. Go ahead and cry. The passion I see in your eyes is contagious for now my eyes are watering. Is your master coming?

Servant

He lies tonight within seven leagues of Rome.

He is with seven Roman battalions tonight.

Antony

Post back with speed, and tell him what hath chanced. Here is a mourning Rome, a dangerous Rome, No Rome of safety for Octavius yet; Hie hence, and tell him so. Yet stay awhile; Thou shalt not back till I have borne this corse Into the market-place: there shall I try, In my oration, how the people take The cruel issue of these bloody men; According to the which thou shalt discourse To young Octavius of the state of things. Lend me your hand.

Go back quickly and tell him what has happened. Rome is dangerous and not safe for Octavius, yet. No, stay awhile. Don't leave until I take the body to the market-place. We will see how the people respond to this bloody event. Then you can let Octavius know how things are. Give me a hand.

Exit with Caesar's body.

Scene II: The forum.

Enter Brutus, Cassius, and a throng of Citizens

Citizens

We will be satisfied; let us be satisfied.

Tell us something to satisfy us.

Brutus

Then follow me, and give me audience, friends.-- Cassius, go you into the other street And part the numbers.-- Those that will hear me speak, let 'em stay here; Those that will follow Cassius, go with him; And public reasons shall be rendered Of Caesar's death.

Then follow me and listen, friends. Cassius, go part the crowds. Those who want to hear me speak, stay. Everyone else, go with Cassius. We will explain the reasons for Caesar's death.

First Citizen

I will hear Brutus speak.

I want to hear Brutus speak.

Second Citizen

I will hear Cassius; and compare their reasons, When severally we hear them rendered.

I will listen to Cassius, so we can compare their reasons.

Exit Cassius with some of the Citizens. Brutus goes into the pulpit.

Third Citizen

The noble Brutus is ascended: silence!

The noble Brutus is ready. Silence!

Brutus

Be patient till the last. Romans, countrymen, and lovers! Hear me for my cause; and be silent, that you may hear: believe me for mine honour, and have respect to mine honor, that you may believe: censure me in your wisdom; and awake your senses, that you may the better judge. If there be any in this assembly, any dear friend of Caesar's, to him I say that Brutus' love to Caesar was no less than his. If then that friend demand why Brutus rose against Caesar, this is my answer,--Not that I loved Caesar less, but that I loved Rome more. Had you rather Caesar were living, and die all slaves, than that Caesar were dead, to live all freemen? As Caesar loved me, I weep for him; as he was fortunate, I rejoice at it; as he was valiant, I honour him; but, as he was ambitious, I slew him. There is tears for his love; joy for his fortune; honour for his valour; and death for his ambition. Who is here so base that would be a bondman? If any, speak; for him have I offended. Who is here so rude that would not be a Roman? If any, speak; for him have I offended. Who is here so vile that will not love his country? If any, speak; for him have I offended. I pause for a reply.

Please hear me out. Romans, countrymen, and lovers of Caesar, be quiet and listen to what I have to say. By my honor, believe me I loved Caesar as well as anyone. You are probably wondering why I rose against him. My reason is this, I loved Rome more. Ask yourself, if you had rather Caesar lived and die as a slave or had Caesar dead and live as free men. For his love, I wept for him. He was a fortunate man, and I rejoiced in his fortune. He was brave, and I honored him. But, he was ambitious, so I killed him. If there is anyone here whom I have offended, then you are not a true Roman. Is there anyone who wants to speak against their country? I'm waiting.

All

None, Brutus, none.

None, Brutus, none.

Brutus

Then none have I offended. I have done no more to Caesar than you shall do to Brutus. The question of his death is enroll'd in the Capitol, his glory not extenuated, wherein he was worthy;, nor his offenses enforced, for which he suffered death.

Then I haven't offended anyone. I have done no more to Caesar than you would do to me. Now you know the reasons for his death. He was a man worthy of glory, but his offences for which he died could not be tolerated.

Enter Antony and others with Caesar's body.

Here comes his body, mourned by Mark Antony, who, though he had no hand in his death, shall receive the benefit of his dying, a place in the commonwealth; as which of you shall not? With this I depart-- that, as I slew my best lover for the good of Rome, I have the same dagger for myself, when it shall please my country to need my death.

Here comes his body, carried by Mark Antony, who had no part in his death but will benefit by taking a place in the senate. Is there anyone who objects? Now, I will depart saying I killed my best friend for the good of Rome. I hold the same dagger for myself, if it is for the good of Rome.

All

Live, Brutus! live, live!

Live, Brutus, live, live!

First Citizen

Bring him with triumph home unto his house.

Take him home with triumph.

Second Citizen

Give him a statue with his ancestors.

Erect a statue in his honor.

Third Citizen

Let him be Caesar.

Let him be Caesar.

Fourth Citizen

Caesar's better parts Shall be crown'd in Brutus.

Let him be crowned as an equal to Caesar.

First Citizen

We'll bring him to his house with shouts and clamours.

Let's carry him to his house and shout in victory.

Brutus

My countrymen,--

My countrymen…

Second Citizen

Peace! silence! Brutus speaks.

Be quiet! Silence! Brutus speaks.

First Citizen

Peace, ho!

Be quiet!

Brutus

Good countrymen, let me depart alone, And, for my sake, stay here with Antony: Do grace to Caesar's corpse, and grace his speech Tending to Caesar's glory; which Mark Antony, By our permission, is allow'd to make. I do entreat you, not a man depart, Save I alone, till Antony have spoke.

My good countrymen, let me depart alone. Stay here with Antony and honor Caesar's body and listen to Antony's speech glorifying Caesar. We are allowing Mark Antony to speak, so I'm asking that you stay until Antony is finished.

Exit.

First Citizen

Stay, ho! and let us hear Mark Antony.

Stay everyone! Let's listen to Mark Antony.

Third Citizen

Let him go up into the public chair; We'll hear him.--Noble Antony, go up.

Let him go up to the podium. We'll listen to him. Go on, noble Antony.

Antony

For Brutus' sake, I am beholding to you.

For Brutus's sake, I will.

Goes into the pulpit.

Fourth Citizen

What does he say of Brutus?

What did he say about Brutus?

Third Citizen

He says, for Brutus' sake, He finds himself beholding to us all.

He said he was going to speak for Brutus's sake and he owed it to us.

Fourth Citizen

'Twere best he speak no harm of Brutus here.

He better not talk poorly about Brutus here.

First Caesar

This Caesar was a tyrant.

This Caesar was a tyrant.

Third Citizen

Nay, that's certain: We are blest that Rome is rid of him.

That's for sure. We are blessed that Rome is rid of him.

Second Citizen

Peace! let us hear what Antony can say.

Be quiet! Let's hear what Antony has to say.

Antony

You gentle Romans,--

Gentle Romans…

Citizens

Peace, ho! let us hear him.

Silence! Let's hear what he has to say.

Antony

Friends, Romans, countrymen, lend me your ears; I come to bury Caesar, not to praise him. The evil that men do lives after them; The good is oft interred with their bones: So let it be with Caesar. The noble Brutus Hath told you Caesar was ambitious: If it were so, it was a grievous fault; And grievously hath Caesar answer'd it. Here, under leave of Brutus and the rest,-- For Brutus is an honourable man; So are they all, all honorable men,-- Come I to speak in Caesar's funeral. He was my friend, faithful and just to me: But Brutus says he was ambitious; And Brutus is an honourable man. He hath brought many captives home to Rome, Whose ransoms did the general coffers fill: Did this in Caesar seem ambitious? When that the poor have cried, Caesar hath wept: Ambition should be made of sterner stuff: Yet Brutus says he was ambitious; And Brutus is an honourable man. You all did see that on the Lupercal I thrice presented him a kingly crown, Which he did thrice refuse: was this ambition? Yet Brutus says he was ambitious; And, sure, he is an honourable man. I speak not to disprove what Brutus spoke, But here I am to speak what I do know. You all did love him once,--not without cause: What cause withholds you, then, to mourn for him?-- O judgment, thou art fled to brutish beasts, And men have lost their reason!--Bear with me; My heart is in the coffin there with Caesar, And I must pause till it come back to me.

Friends, Romans, and countrymen, listen to me. I have come to bury Caesar, not to praise him. The evil men do doesn't die with them, but the good is often buried with them. So, it will be true of Caesar. Brutus has told you of Caesar's ambition, and he is noble man. He has brought many prisoners home to Rome whose ransoms filled Rome's banks. Did Caesar seem ambitious when the he cried with the poor? Yet, Brutus said Caesar was ambitious, and Brutus is an honorable man. You all saw at the Lupercal I offered the crown to Caesar three times, and he refused each time. Did this seem like ambition? Yet, honorable Brutus said he was. I am not speaking to disagree with Brutus. I only speak of what I know. You all loved Caesar once and not without cause. Why aren't you mourning for him, now? Let you be judged as beasts without reason. Give me a moment; my heart is with Caesar. I must pause a moment until it comes back to me.

First Citizen

Methinks there is much reason in his sayings.

He makes a lot of sense.

Second Citizen

If thou consider rightly of the matter, Caesar has had great wrong.

If you think about it, Caesar has been wronged.

Third Citizen

Has he not, masters? I fear there will a worse come in his place.

I'm afraid someone worse than him will take his place.

Fourth Citizen

Mark'd ye his words? He would not take the crown; Therefore 'tis certain he was not ambitious.

Listen to his words. He refused the crown; therefore, he was not ambitious.

First Citizen

If it be found so, some will dear abide it.

Some will agree to that.

Second Citizen

Poor soul! his eyes are red as fire with weeping.

Poor man! Look at Antony's eyes. They are as red as fire from crying.

Third Citizen

There's not a nobler man in Rome than Antony.

There is not a nobler man than Antony in all of Rome.

Fourth Citizen

Now mark him; he begins again to speak.

Listen! He is starting to speak again.

Antony

But yesterday the word of Caesar might Have stood against the world: now lies he there, And none so poor to do him reverence. O masters, if I were disposed to stir Your hearts and minds to mutiny and rage, I should do Brutus wrong and Cassius wrong, Who, you all know, are honourable men: I will not do them wrong; I rather choose To wrong the dead, to wrong myself, and you, Than I will wrong such honourable men. But here's a parchment with the seal of Caesar,-- I found it in his closet,--'tis his will: Let but the commons hear this testament,-- Which, pardon me, I do not mean to read,-- And they would go and kiss dead Caesar's wounds, And dip their napkins in his sacred blood; Yea, beg a hair of him for memory, And, dying, mention it within their wills, Bequeathing it as a rich legacy Unto their issue.

Yesterday, Caesar's words would have stood up against any in the world. Now, he lies there, and no one is revering him. If I caused you men to be angry with honorable Brutus and Cassius, I would do them a wrong, as well as you and myself. Here's the will of Caesar, I found in his study. If you could hear his last will and testament, you would kiss Caesar's wounds and beg for a hair to remember him by, which you would leave as a legacy in your will to pass down. I don't mean to read it though.

First Citizen

We'll hear the will: read it, Mark Antony.

We'll hear it. Read it Mark Antony!

All

The will, the will! We will hear Caesar's will.

The will! The will! We want to hear Caesar's will!

Antony

Have patience, gentle friends, I must not read it; It is not meet you know how Caesar loved you. You are not wood, you are not stones, but men; And, being men, hearing the will of Caesar, It will inflame you, it will make you mad. 'Tis good you know not that you are his heirs; For if you should, O, what would come of it!

Gentle friends, be patient. I mustn't read it. You shouldn't know how much Caesar loved you. You are not made of wood or stone, and if you hear it, you will be angry. You should not hear that you were his heirs. I am scared to think what would happen next!

Fourth Citizen

Read the will! we'll hear it, Antony; You shall read us the will,--Caesar's will!

Read the will. We want to hear it, Antony. Read us the will of Caesar.

Antony

Will you be patient? will you stay awhile? I have o'ershot myself to tell you of it: I fear I wrong the honorable men Whose daggers have stabb'd Caesar; I do fear it.

Will you be patient and stay a little longer? I shouldn't have told you about it. I am afraid I have caused harm to the honorable men who killed Caesar.

Fourth Citizen

They were traitors: honourable men!

Honorable men! They were traitors.

All

The will! The testament!

The will! The testament!

Second Citizen

They were villains, murderers. The will! read the will!

They were villains! Murderers! Read the will.

Antony

You will compel me, then, to read the will? Then make a ring about the corpse of Caesar, And let me show you him that made the will. Shall I descend? and will you give me leave?

You will force to read the will? Then, make a ring around Caesar's body, and let me show you who wrote it. Let me come down. Make way.

Several Citizens

Come down.

Come down.

Second Citizen

Descend.

Come down.

Third Citizen

You shall have leave.

We will make way.

Antony comes down.

Fourth Citizen

A ring! stand round.

Make a ring around the body.

First Citizen

Stand from the hearse, stand from the body.

Stand around the body.

SECOND CITIZEN

Room for Antony!--most noble Antony!

Antony

Nay, press not so upon me; stand far' off.

Give me some room. Stand back.

Several Citizens

Stand back; room! bear back.

Stand back. Make room.

Antony

If you have tears, prepare to shed them now. You all do know this mantle: I remember The first time ever Caesar put it on; 'Twas on a Summer's evening, in his tent, That day he overcame the Nervii. Look, in this place ran Cassius' dagger through: See what a rent the envious Casca made: Through this the well-beloved Brutus stabb'd; And as he pluck'd his cursed steel away, Mark how the blood of Caesar follow'd it,-- As rushing out of doors, to be resolved If Brutus so unkindly knock'd, or no; For Brutus, as you know, was Caesar's angel: Judge, O you gods, how dearly Caesar loved him! This was the most unkindest cut of all; For when the noble Caesar saw him stab, Ingratitude, more strong than traitors' arms, Quite vanquish'd him: then burst his mighty heart; And, in his mantle muffling up his face, Even at the base of Pompey's statua, Which all the while ran blood, great Caesar fell. O, what a fall was there, my countrymen! Then I, and you, and all of us fell down, Whilst bloody treason flourish'd over us. O, now you weep; and, I perceive, you feel The dint of pity: these are gracious drops. Kind souls, what, weep you when you but behold Our Caesar's vesture wounded? Look you here, Here is himself, marr'd, as you see, with traitors.

If you have any tears, prepare to shed them now. You all know this robe. I remember the first time I saw him put it on. It was on a summer's evening in his tent the day he conquered Nervii. Look, this is where Cassius's dagger went through his body. See the whole Casca made. Here is where the beloved Brutus stabbed him and pulled his sword out. Look at how Caesar's blood rushed out as if to ask for forgiveness. Brutus, Caesar's angel, because you know how much Caesar loved him, caused the deadliest cut of all. The cut of ingratitude burst his heart. Great Caesar died at the base of Pompey's statue, where all his blood flowed out. I see you are touched and weep for him now, while you see what the traitors did to him.

First Citizen

O piteous spectacle!

What a pitiful sight!

Second Citizen

O noble Caesar!

Oh, noble Caesar!

Third Citizen

O woeful day!

What a terrible day!

Fourth Citizen

O traitors, villains!

Oh, traitors! Villains!

First Citizen

O most bloody sight!

This is the bloodiest sight!

Second Citizen

We will be revenged.

We will seek revenge.

All

Revenge,--about,--seek,--burn,--fire,--kill,--slay,--let not a traitor live!

Revenge! Burn! Fire! Kill! Let not one traitor live!

Antony

Stay, countrymen.

Stop, countrymen.

First Citizen

Peace there! hear the noble Antony.

Be quiet! Listen to the noble Antony.

Second Citizen

We'll hear him, we'll follow him, we'll die with him.

Let's hear him and follow him. We'll die with him.

Antony

Good friends, sweet friends, let me not stir you up To such a sudden flood of mutiny. They that have done this deed are honourable: What private griefs they have, alas, I know not, That made them do it; they're wise and honourable, And will, no doubt, with reasons answer you. I come not, friends, to steal away your hearts: I am no orator, as Brutus is; But, as you know me all, a plain blunt man, That love my friend; and that they know full well That gave me public leave to speak of him: For I have neither wit, nor words, nor worth, Action, nor utterance, nor the power of speech, To stir men's blood: I only speak right on; I tell you that which you yourselves do know; Show you sweet Caesar's wounds, poor dumb mouths, And bid them speak for me: but were I Brutus, And Brutus Antony, there were an Antony Would ruffle up your spirits, and put a tongue In every wound of Caesar, that should move The stones of Rome to rise and mutiny.

Good friends, don't let me stir you up to the point of mutiny. Those who committed this act are honorable men with private grief. I don't know why they did it, but they are wise and honorable, and will give you their reasons. Don't let me change your hearts. I'm no orator like Brutus. I am just a plain man who loved his friend, and they allowed me to speak here today. I am not capable of stirring me to action. I'm only here to tell you what happened and show you Caesar's wounds, which speak for themselves. If I were Brutus, I might be able to cause a stir among you.

All

We'll mutiny.

We'll mutiny.

First Citizen

We'll burn the house of Brutus.

We'll burn the house of Brutus.

Third Citizen

Away, then! come, seek the conspirators.

Let's go! Seek the conspirators.

Antony

Yet hear me, countrymen; yet hear me speak.

Listen to me countrymen. Hear me speak.

All

Peace, ho! hear Antony; most noble Antony!

Shh! Listen to Antony! Most noble Antony!

Antony

Why, friends, you go to do you know not what. Wherein hath Caesar thus deserved your loves? Alas, you know not; I must tell you then: You have forgot the will I told you of.

You don't know what you are doing. You must know how Caesar deserved your love. You have forgotten about the will.

All

Most true; the will!--let's stay, and hear the will.

True! The will! Let's stay and hear the will.

Antony

Here is the will, and under Caesar's seal. To every Roman citizen he gives, To every several man, seventy-five drachmas.

Here is the will bearing Caesar's seal. to every Roman citizen he gives seventy-five drachmas.

Second Citizen

Most noble Caesar!--we'll revenge his death.

Most noble Caesar! We'll revenge your death.

Third Citizen

O, royal Caesar!

Oh, royal Caesar!

Antony

Hear me with patience.

Listen to me. Be patient.

All

Peace, ho!

Be quiet!

Antony

Moreover, he hath left you all his walks, His private arbors, and new-planted orchards, On this side Tiber: he hath left them you, And to your heirs forever; common pleasures, To walk abroad, and recreate yourselves. Here was a Caesar! when comes such another?

He also left you his land, including his trees and orchards on this side of the river Tiber. He has left them to you to enjoy, to walk among, and to pass along to your children. Here was a Caesar! I don't know if there will ever be another.

First Citizen

Never, never.--Come, away, away! We'll burn his body in the holy place, And with the brands fire the traitors' houses. Take up the body.

Never, never! Let's go! We'll burn his body in the holy place, and carry the fire to the traitors' houses. Pick up the body.

Second Citizen

Go, fetch fire.

Go get the fire.

Third Citizen

Pluck down benches.

Get some wood. Take down the benches.

Fourth Citizen

Pluck down forms, windows, any thing.

Take down the window, the doors, anything.

Exit Citizens with the body.

Antony

Now let it work.--Mischief, thou art afoot, Take thou what course thou wilt!--

Now let come what may. Mischief, you are at work. Let your course begin.

Enter a Servant

How now, fellow?

How are you, fellow?

Servant

Sir, Octavius is already come to Rome.

Sir, Octavius is ready to come to Rome.

Antony

Where is he?

Where is he?

Servant

He and Lepidus are at Caesar's house.

He and Lepidus are at Caesar's house.

Antony

And thither will I straight to visit him: He comes upon a wish. Fortune is merry, And in this mood will give us any thing.

I will go visit him. He is an answer to my prayers. Fortune is on our side and will give us whatever we want.

Servant

I heard 'em say Brutus and Cassius Are rid like madmen through the gates of Rome.

I heard him say, Brutus and Cassius are like madmen.

Antony

Belike they had some notice of the people, How I had moved them. Bring me to Octavius.

The people are just as mad. Did you see how I moved them? Bring me to Octavius.

Exit.

Scene III: A street.

Enter Cinna the poet

Cinna the poet

I dreamt to-night that I did feast with Caesar, And things unluckily charge my fantasy: I have no will to wander forth of doors, Yet something leads me forth.

I dreamed tonight that I ate with Caesar,

And unlucky things ran through my fantasy:

I have no desire to enter the door,

Yet, something leads me forward.

Enter Citizens.

First Citizen

What is your name?

What's your name?

Second Citizen

Whither are you going?

Where are you going?

Third Citizen

Where do you dwell?

Where do you live?

Fourth Citizen

Are you a married man or a bachelor?

Are you married or single?

Second Citizen

Answer every man directly.

Answer each man.

First Citizen

Ay, and briefly.

Yes, but brief.

Fourth Citizen

Ay, and wisely.

And choose your words wisely.

Third Citizen

Ay, and truly; you were best.

Yes and be honest.

Cinna the Poet

What is my name? Whither am I going? Where do I dwell? Am I a married man or a bachelor? Then, to answer every man directly and briefly, wisely and truly. Wisely I say I am a bachelor.

What is my name? Where am I going? Where do live? Am I married or single? Well, to answer each of you directly and briefly, wisely and honestly, then I say wisely, "I am a bachelor."

Second Citizen

That's as much as to say they are fools that marry; you'll bear me a bang for that, I fear. Proceed; directly.

Are you saying it is foolish to marry? Careful, you are stepping on my toes. Go on.

Cinna the Poet

Directly, I am going to Caesar's funeral.

Honestly, I am going to Caesar's funeral.

First Citizen

As a friend, or an enemy?

Are you a friend or enemy?

Cinna the Poet

As a friend.

I am a friend.

Second Citizen

That matter is answered directly.

You answered that well.

Fourth Citizen

For your dwelling,--briefly.

And, where do you live? Be brief.

Cinna the Poet

Briefly, I dwell by the Capitol.

I live near the Capitol.

Third Citizen

Your name, sir, truly.

Tell us your name. Don't lie.

Cinna the Poet

Truly, my name is Cinna.

I am Cinna, honestly.

First Citizen

Tear him to pieces! he's a conspirator.

Tear him to pieces for he is one of the conspirators.

Cinna the Poet

I am Cinna the poet, I am Cinna the poet.

I am Cinna the poet! I am Cinna the poet.

Fourth Citizen

Tear him for his bad verses, tear him for his bad verses.

Kill him for his bad verses. Kill him for his bad verses.

Cinna the Poet

I am not Cinna the conspirator.

I am not Cinna the conspirator.

Fourth Citizen

It is no matter, his name's Cinna; pluck but his name out of his heart, and turn him going.

It doesn't matter. His name's Cinna. Pluck his name right out of his heart.

Third Citizen

Tear him, tear him! Come; brands, ho! firebrands. To Brutus', to Cassius'; burn all. Some to Decius' house, and some to Casca's, some to Ligarius': away, go!

Kill him! Kill him! Come, bring your fire. Let's go to Brutus's, Cassius's, and burn them all. Some of you go to Decius's house and some got to Casca's and Ligarius's. Get going!

Exit.

Act IV

Scene I: A house in Rome.

Antony, Octavius, and Lepidus sit at a table.

Antony

These many then shall die; their names are prick'd.

These men will die. Their names are listed.

Octavius

Your brother too must die: consent you, Lepidus?

Your brother must die, too. Are you okay with that, Lepidus?

Lepidus

I do consent,--

I am.

Octavius

Prick him down, Antony.

Write his name down, too, Antony.

Lepidus

--Upon condition Publius shall not live, Who is your sister's son, Mark Antony.

On one condition. Publius, your sister's son, must also die, Mark Antony.

Antony

He shall not live; look, with a spot I damn him. But, Lepidus, go you to Caesar's house; Fetch the will hither, and we shall determine How to cut off some charge in legacies.

He shall not live. Look, I have written down his name to be damned. Lepidus, go to Caesar's house and get his will so we can figure out how to handle it.

Lepidus

What, shall I find you here?

Will you be here when I return?

Octavius

Or here, or at the Capitol.

Here or in the Capitol.

Exit Lepidus.

Antony

This is a slight unmeritable man, Meet to be sent on errands: is it fit, The three-fold world divided, he should stand One of the three to share it?

This man is only fit to be sent on errands. The world is about to be divided. Should he be one of the three to share in this?

Octavius

So you thought him; And took his voice who should be prick'd to die, In our black sentence and proscription.

You thought he was when you started to name the men who should die.

Antony

Octavius, I have seen more days than you: And, though we lay these honors on this man, To ease ourselves of divers slanderous loads, He shall but bear them as the ass bears gold, To groan and sweat under the business, Either led or driven, as we point the way; And having brought our treasure where we will, Then take we down his load and turn him off, Like to the empty ass, to shake his ears And graze in commons.

Octavius, I am older than you, and although, we give this man the job to ease our burden, he will bear it like a donkey bears gold. He will groan and sweat. He will be led or driven, and once we are finished with him, we will take his load and turn him loose to graze in the fields.

Octavius

You may do your will; But he's a tried and valiant soldier.

Do what you want, but he's a honorable and courageous soldier.

Antony

So is my horse, Octavius;and for that I do appoint him store of provender: It is a creature that I teach to fight, To wind, to stop, to run directly on, His corporal motion govern'd by my spirit. And, in some taste, is Lepidus but so; He must be taught, and train'd, and bid go forth: A barren-spirited fellow; one that feeds On objects, arts, and imitations, Which, out of use and staled by other men, Begin his fashion: do not talk of him But as a property. And now, Octavius, Listen great things. Brutus and Cassius Are levying powers: we must straight make head; Therefore let our alliance be combined, Our best friends made, our means stretch'd; And let us presently go sit in council, How covert matters may be best disclosed, And open perils surest answered.

So is my horse, Octavius, and for that I give him food. He is someone who needs to be taught and directed to go forward. He is unspirited and feeds on stale traditions. Now, Octavius, listen. Brutus and Cassius are putting armies together. We must form an alliance and begin to prepare.

Octavius

Let us do so: for we are at the stake, And bay'd about with many enemies; And some that smile have in their hearts, I fear, Millions of mischiefs.

Let's get started for our lives are at stake. We are surrounded by enemies with mischief in their hearts who smile in our face.

Exit.

Scene II: Camp near Sardis. Before Brutus's tent.

Drum. Enter Brutus, Lucilius, Lucius, and Soldiers. Titinius and Pindarus meet them.

Brutus

Stand, ho!

Stop!

Lucilius

Give the word, ho! and stand.

Tell everyone to stop!

Brutus

What now, Lucilius! is Cassius near?

What's going on, Lucilius? Is Cassius nearby?

Lucilius

He is at hand; and Pindarus is come To do you salutation from his master.

He's nearby, and Pindarus has come to greet you on his behalf.

Brutus

He greets me well.--Your master, Pindarus, In his own change, or by ill officers, Hath given me some worthy cause to wish Things done, undone: but, if he be at hand, I shall be satisfied.

Pindarus, you are a good man, but your master has either changed his mind or been influenced by bad officers. I wish we hadn't done some of the things we did. I need an explanation.

Pindarus

I do not doubt But that my noble master will appear Such as he is, full of regard and honour.

I don't doubt that my noble master will show up.

Brutus

He is not doubted.--A word, Lucilius: How he received you, let me be resolved.

I don't doubt him. Lucilius, I need to ask how Cassius received you.

Lucilius

With courtesy and with respect enough; But not with such familiar instances, Nor with such free and friendly conference, As he hath used of old.

He treated me courteously and with respect, but he wasn't friendly like he is usually.

Brutus

Thou hast described A hot friend cooling: ever note, Lucilius, When love begins to sicken and decay, It useth an enforced ceremony. There are no tricks in plain and simple faith; But hollow men, like horses hot at hand, Make gallant show and promise of their mettle; But, when they should endure the bloody spur, They fall their crests, and, like deceitful jades Sink in the trial. Comes his army on?

You have just described a friend in retreat. Remember, Lucilius, when someone no longer wants to be your friend, they act as you have described. Hollow men are like showy horses. They look gallant, but when it's time to work, they disappear. Is his army coming?

Lucilius

They meant his night in Sard is to be quarter'd: The greater part, the Horse in general, Are come with Cassius.

They are in Sardis tonight to be dispersed. The largest is coming with Cassius.

Brutus

Hark! he is arrived. March gently on to meet him.

Listen! He is here.

Low march within.

Let's go to meet him.

Enter Cassius and his men.

Cassius

Stand, ho!

Stop!

Brutus

Stand, ho! Speak the word along.

Stop! Tell the others.

First Soldier

Stand!

Stop!

Second Soldier

Stand!

Stop!

Third Soldier

Stand!

Stop!

Cassius

Most noble brother, you have done me wrong.

Most noble brother, you have done me wrong.

Brutus

Judge me, you gods! wrong I mine enemies? And, if not so, how should I wrong a brother?

Let the gods judge me, if I have done you wrong. How I have I wronged you?

Cassius

Brutus, this sober form of yours hides wrongs; And when you do them--

You may act like you haven't done anything, but you know you...

Brutus

Cassius, be content; Speak your griefs softly, I do know you well. Before the eyes of both our armies here, Which should perceive nothing but love from us, Let us not wrangle; bid them move away; Then in my tent, Cassius, enlarge your griefs, And I will give you audience.

Cassius, calm down. Tell me what's bothering you calmly. I know you very well. In front of both our armies, who should see nothing but love from us, let's not fight. Tell them to move on, and we'll go in my tent, so I can hear what you have to say.

Cassius

Pindarus, Bid our commanders lead their charges off A little from this ground.

Pindarus, tell the commanders to fall back.

Brutus

Lucilius, do you the like; and let no man Come to our tent till we have done our conference.-- Lucius and Titinius, guard our door.

Lucilius, you do the same, and don't let anyone come to my tent until we are done conferencing. Let Lucius and Titinius guard the door.

Exit.

Scene III: Brutus's tent.

Enter Brutus and Cassius

Cassius

That you have wrong'd me doth appear in this: You have condemn'd and noted Lucius Pella For taking bribes here of the Sardians; Whereas my letters, praying on his side Because I knew the man, were slighted off.

You wronged me when you condemned Lucius Pella for taking bribes from the Sardians. You ignored my letters on his behalf. I knew the man.

Brutus

You wrong'd yourself to write in such a case.

You were wrong to write those letters.

Cassius

In such a time as this it is not meet That every nice offense should bear his comment.

In times like these, you shouldn't talk about others offences.

Brutus

Let me tell you, Cassius, you yourself Are much condemn'd to have an itching palm, To sell and mart your offices for gold To undeservers.

You are one to talk when you sell your offices for to people who don't deserve them.

Cassius

I an itching palm! You know that you are Brutus that speak this, Or, by the gods, this speech were else your last.

Are you calling me greedy? If anybody else made such a claim against me, it would be their last.

Brutus

The name of Cassius honors this corruption, And chastisement doth therefore hide his head.

You use your name to cover up corruption.

Cassius

Chastisement!

Corruption!

Brutus

Remember March, the Ides of March remember: Did not great Julius bleed for justice' sake? What villain touch'd his body, that did stab, And not for justice? What! shall one of us, That struck the foremost man of all this world But for supporting robbers,--shall we now Contaminate our fingers with base bribes And sell the mighty space of our large honours For so much trash as may be grasped thus? I had rather be a dog, and bay the moon, Than such a Roman.

Remember in March, March 15th? Didn't the great Julius bleed for the sake of justice? Who stabbed him who was not seeking justice? Didn't we kill him for supporting robbers? Should we begin to do the same thing? I rather be a dog and howl at the moon than a Roman like that.

Cassius

Brutus, bay not me, I'll not endure it: you forget yourself, To hedge me in; I am a soldier, ay, Older in practice, abler than yourself To make conditions.

Don't howl at me, Brutus. I won't take it. You've forgotten who you are talking to. I am a soldier, and much wiser than you, and more able to make things happen.

Brutus

Go to; you are not, Cassius.

Go for it. You are not the Cassius, I used to know.

Cassius

I am.

Oh, yes I am.

Brutus

I say you are not.

Well, I say you aren't.

Cassius

Urge me no more, I shall forget myself; Have mind upon your health, tempt me no farther.

You better stop, before I forget myself. Remember your health and don't tempt me.

Brutus

Away, slight man!

Get out of here, little man!

Cassius

Is't possible?

Oh, yeah?

Brutus

Hear me, for I will speak. Must I give way and room to your rash choler? Shall I be frighted when a madman stares?

You better listen to what I'm saying. I will not be frightened by you.

Cassius

O gods, ye gods! must I endure all this?

Oh, gods! Must I endure this?

Brutus

All this? ay, more: fret till your proud heart break; Go show your slaves how choleric you are, And make your bondmen tremble. Must I budge? Must I observe you? Must I stand and crouch Under your testy humour? By the gods, You shall digest the venom of your spleen, Though it do split you; for, from this day forth, I'll use you for my mirth, yea, for my laughter, When you are waspish.

Yes! This and more! You can worry until your heart breaks. Why don't you go show your slaves how sick you are and try to make them scared? You won't do that to me. Do you expect me to cower in your presence? You will die first. From this day forward, I will use you for comic relief.

Cassius

Is it come to this?

So this is what it's come to?

Brutus

You say you are a better soldier: Let it appear so; make your vaunting true, And it shall please me well: for mine own part, I shall be glad to learn of abler men.

You say you are a better soldier. Prove it.

Cassius

You wrong me every way, you wrong me, Brutus. I said, an elder soldier, not a better: Did I say "better"?

How dare you! I said, "I was a wiser solder, not a better one."

Brutus

If you did, I care not.

Whatever.

Cassius

When Caesar lived, he durst not thus have moved me.

Caesar never made me this angry when he lived.

Brutus

Peace, peace! you durst not so have tempted him.

You dared not treat him like this.

Cassius

I durst not?

I dared not!

Brutus

No.

No.

Cassius

What, durst not tempt him?

I dared not anger him!

Brutus

For your life you durst not.

You feared for your life, so you didn't dare.

Cassius

Do not presume too much upon my love; I may do that I shall be sorry for.

You assume too much based on my love for you. You may force me to do something I will be sorry for.

Brutus

You have done that you should be sorry for. There is no terror, Cassius, in your threats, For I am arm'd so strong in honesty, That they pass by me as the idle wind Which I respect not. I did send to you For certain sums of gold, which you denied me;-- For I can raise no money by vile means: By Heaven, I had rather coin my heart, And drop my blood for drachmas, than to wring From the hard hands of peasants their vile trash By any indirection:--I did send To you for gold to pay my legions, Which you denied me: was that done like Cassius? Should I have answer'd Caius Cassius so? When Marcus Brutus grows so covetous To lock such rascal counters from his friends, Be ready, gods, with all your thunderbolts, Dash him to pieces!

You already have, and I am not afraid of your threats. Your idle threats go right by me. I sent you a request for money to pay for my army, and you denied me. Should I have resorted to steal from my friends to pay for my men, like you? May the gods curse me with their thunderbolts and tear me to pieces, if I do that!

Cassius

I denied you not.

I didn't deny you.

Brutus

You did.

Yes, you did.

Cassius

I did not. He was but a fool That brought my answer back. Brutus hath rived my heart: A friend should bear his friend's infirmities, But Brutus makes mine greater than they are.

I did not. My messenger must have been a fool when he delivered my answer. You have broken my heart. You should know me better than that. I am full of faults, but I would never do that to you.

Brutus

I do not, till you practise them on me.

I didn't think so, until you used them against me.

Cassius

You love me not.

You don't love me.

Brutus

I do not like your faults.

I don't like your faults.

Cassius

A friendly eye could never see such faults.

A friend would not see such faults.

Brutus

A flatterer's would not, though they do appear As huge as high Olympus.

I am your friend, not your slave, and your faults are as great as Mount Olympus.

Cassius

Come, Antony and young Octavius, come, Revenge yourselves alone on Cassius, For Cassius is a-weary of the world; Hated by one he loves; braved by his brother; Check'd like a bondman; all his faults observed, Set in a note-book, learn'd and conn'd by rote, To cast into my teeth. O, I could weep My spirit from mine eyes!--There is my dagger, And here my naked breast; within, a heart Dearer than Plutus' mine, richer than gold: If that thou be'st a Roman, take it forth; I, that denied thee gold, will give my heart: Strike as thou didst at Caesar; for I know, When thou didst hate him worst, thou lovedst him better Than ever thou lovedst Cassius.

Come, Antony and young Octavius are coming. You must fight them alone, because I am tired of this world. I am hated by someone I love. My faults have been listed and remembered to be thrown back in my face. Take this dagger and plunge it into my chest. Remove my heart, Roman, which is more valuable than Pluto's silver, if I denied you money. Kill me like you did Caesar, because I know you know you loved him better than me.

Brutus

Sheathe your dagger: Be angry when you will, it shall have scope; Do what you will, dishonor shall be humour. O Cassius, you are yoked with a lamb That carries anger as the flint bears fire; Who, much enforced, shows a hasty spark, And straight is cold again.

Put your dagger away. Be angry later, when it's time to be angry. You are like a lamb and I am like a flint with fire when it comes to carrying anger, here one minute and gone the next.

Cassius

Hath Cassius lived To be but mirth and laughter to his Brutus, When grief, and blood ill-temper'd, vexeth him?

Am I just a cause to laugh at, Brutus, when you are angry?

Brutus

When I spoke that, I was ill-temper'd too.

I was angry when I said that.

Cassius

Do you confess so much? Give me your hand.

You admit it then? Give me your hand.

Brutus

And my heart too.

Take my hand and my heart, too.

Cassius

O Brutus,--

Oh, Brutus!

Brutus

What's the matter?

What's wrong?

Cassius

--Have not you love enough to bear with me, When that rash humor which my mother gave me Makes me forgetful?

Do you love me enough to forgive me when my faults are inherited from my mother?

Brutus

Yes, Cassius; and from henceforth, When you are over-earnest with your Brutus, He'll think your mother chides, and leave you so.

Yes, Cassius, and from now on when you are acting like this with me, I'll blame your mother.

Poet

Within.

Let me go in to see the generals: There is some grudge between 'em; 'tis not meet They be alone.

Let me in to see the generals. They shouldn't be alone.

Lucilius

[Within.] You shall not come to them.

You can't go in.

Poet

[Within.] Nothing but death shall stay me.

You'll have to kill me to stop me.

Enter Poet, followed by Lucilius, Titinius, and Lucius.

Cassius

How now! What's the matter?

Hey! What's the matter?

Poet

For shame, you generals! what do you mean? Love, and be friends, as two such men should be; For I have seen more years, I'm sure, than ye.

Shame on you generals for letting something come between such good friends.

Cassius

Ha, ha! How vilely doth this cynic rhyme!

Ha ha! This man is a terrible poet.

Brutus

Get you hence, sirrah; saucy fellow, hence!

Get out of here, you silly man!

Cassius

Bear with him, Brutus; 'tis his fashion.

Be patient with him, Brutus. That's just how he is.

Brutus

I'll know his humor when he knows his time: What should the wars do with these jigging fools?-- Companion, hence!

He should know when to be humorous. What is he doing here during a war? Companion?

Cassius

Away, away, be gone!

You better go! Go on!

Exit Poet.

Brutus

Lucilius and Titinius, bid the commanders Prepare to lodge their companies tonight.

Lucilius and Titinius tell the commanders to prepare their companies to stay tonight.

Cassius

And come yourselves and bring Messala with you Immediately to us.

Go get Messala and come back to us immediately.

Brutus

Lucius, a bowl of wine!

Lucius, bring me a glass of wine.

Exit Lucius.

Cassius

I did not think you could have been so angry.

I didn't think you could get so angry.

Brutus

O Cassius, I am sick of many griefs.

Oh Cassius, I am sick with grief.

Cassius

Of your philosophy you make no use, If you give place to accidental evils.

I thought your philosophy was to not let things like this bother you.

Brutus

No man bears sorrow better. Portia is dead.

I have more to be sorrowful about; Portia is dead.

Cassius

Ha! Portia!

No way! Portia!

Brutus

She is dead.

She is dead.

Cassius

How 'scaped I killing, when I cross'd you so?-- O insupportable and touching loss!-- Upon what sickness?

How did I escape being killed when I angered you? What a terrible loss! Was she sick?

Brutus

Impatient of my absence, And grief that young Octavius with Mark Antony Have made themselves so strong;-- for with her death That tidings came;--with this she fell distract, And, her attendants absent, swallow'd fire.

She was sick with worry about me being gone and the strong armies led by Octavius and Mark Antony, so she became depressed and she swallowed fire.

Cassius

And died so?

And it killed her?

Brutus

Even so.

Yes.

Cassius

O ye immortal gods!

Oh, immortal gods!

Re-enter Lucius, with wine and candle.

Brutus

Speak no more of her.--Give me a bowl of wine.-- In this I bury all unkindness, Cassius.

Let's not talk of her anymore. Give me the glass of wine. Let's drink and let bygones be bygones, Cassius.

Cassius

My heart is thirsty for that noble pledge. Fill, Lucius, till the wine o'erswell the cup; I cannot drink too much of Brutus' love.

I agree. Fill up the cup, Lucius. I can't get enough of Brutus's love.

Brutus

Come in, Titinius!--

Come in, Titinius!

Exit Lucius.

Re-enter Titinius with Messala.

Welcome, good Messala.-- Now sit we close about this taper here, And call in question our necessities.

Welcome, Messala. Sit with us and let's figure out what we need.

Cassius

Portia, art thou gone?

Oh Portia, are you gone?

Brutus

No more, I pray you.-- Messala, I have here received letters, That young Octavius and Mark Antony Come down upon us with a mighty power, Bending their expedition toward Philippi.

Don't say anything else, please. Messala, I have letters here saying Octavius and Mark Antony are coming down on us with a huge army by way of Philippi.

Messala

Myself have letters of the selfsame tenour.

I have letters with the same message.

Brutus

With what addition?

Do they say anything else?

Messala

That by proscription and bills of outlawry Octavius, Antony, and Lepidus Have put to death an hundred Senators.

It says they have put to death a hundred senators.

Brutus

There in our letters do not well agree: Mine speak of seventy Senators that died By their proscriptions, Cicero being one.

My letters say about seventy senators were killed, one being Cicero.

Cassius

Cicero one!

Cicero was killed!

Messala

Cicero is dead, And by that order of proscription.-- Had you your letters from your wife, my lord?

He is dead. Have you received your letters from your wife, my lord?

Brutus

No, Messala.

No, Messala.

Messala

Nor nothing in your letters writ of her?

And, you haven't heard anything of her in your letters?

Brutus

Nothing, Messala.

Nothing, Messala.

Messala

That, methinks, is strange.

That's strange.

Brutus

Why ask you? hear you aught of her in yours?

Why? Have you heard something?

Messala

No, my lord.

No, my lord.

Brutus

Now, as you are a Roman, tell me true.

Tell me the truth, as a Roman.

Messala

Then like a Roman bear the truth I tell: For certain she is dead, and by strange manner.

Then, like a Roman, she is dead, but by a strange manner.

Brutus

Why, farewell, Portia. We must die, Messala: With meditating that she must die once, I have the patience to endure it now.

Well, farewell, Portia. We must all die, Messala. I have dealt with it once. I have the patience to endure it now.

Messala

Even so great men great losses should endure.

Great men have to endure great losses.

Cassius

I have as much of this in art as you, But yet my nature could not bear it so.

I don't think I could bear it.

Brutus

Well, to our work alive. What do you think Of marching to Philippi presently?

Well, back to work. What do you think about us marching to Philippi now?

Cassius

I do not think it good.

I don't think it's a good idea.

Brutus

Your reason?

Why not?

Cassius

This it is: 'Tis better that the enemy seek us;: So shall he waste his means, weary his soldiers, Doing himself offense; whilst we, lying still, Are full of rest, defense, and nimbleness.

Because I think the enemy should pursue us and wear out his soldiers. In the meantime, we sit and wait, full of rested men ready to fight.

Brutus

Good reasons must, of force, give place to better. The people 'twixt Philippi and this ground Do stand but in a forced affection; For they have grudged us contribution: The enemy, marching along by them, By them shall make a fuller number up, Come on refresh'd, new-added, and encouraged; From which advantage shall we cut him off, If at Philippi we do face him there, These people at our back.

That's a good reason, but there may be a better one to move us forward. Between here and Philippi, they stand a chance of adding men to their regimen. If we meet them, we cut that chance off.

Cassius

Hear me, good brother.

Listen, brother.

Brutus

Under your pardon. You must note besides, That we have tried the utmost of our friends, Our legions are brim-full, our cause is ripe: The enemy increaseth every day; We, at the height, are ready to decline. There is a tide in the affairs of men Which, taken at the flood, leads on to fortune; Omitted, all the voyage of their life Is bound in shallows and in miseries. On such a full sea are we now afloat; And we must take the current when it serves, Or lose our ventures.

I beg your pardon, but you must remember our armies are full and ready. The enemy is increasing every day. We must act quickly while the time is right.

Cassius

Then, with your will, go on: We'll along ourselves, and meet them at Philippi.

Then, we will go and meet them at Philippi.

Brutus

The deep of night is crept upon our talk, And nature must obey necessity; Which we will niggard with a little rest. There is no more to say?

It's night now, so we better rest. Anything else?

Cassius

No more. Good night: Early to-morrow will we rise, and hence.

No more. Goodnight. We will begin early in the morning.

Brutus

Lucius!--My gown.--Farewell now, good Messala:-- Good night, Titinius:--noble, noble Cassius, Good night, and good repose.

Lucius!

Enter Lucius.

Bring me my gown.

Exit Lucius.

Goodbye, Messala. Goodnight, Titinius. Noble Cassius, goodnight and sleep well.

Cassius

O my dear brother! This was an ill beginning of the night. Never come such division 'tween our souls! Let it not, Brutus.

Oh, my dear brother. We had a rough start tonight. May nothing ever come between us, Brutus.

Brutus

Every thing is well.

All is well.

Cassius

Good night, my lord.

Goodnight, my lord.

Brutus

Good night, good brother.

Goodnight, my good brother.

Titinius and Messala

Good night, Lord Brutus.

Goodnight, Lord Brutus.

Brutus

Farewell, everyone.--

Farewell, everyone.

Exit all but Brutus.

Re-enter Lucius with the gown.

Give me the gown. Where is thy instrument?

Give me the gown. Where is your instrument?

Lucius

Here in the tent.

Here in the tent.

Brutus

What, thou speak'st drowsily: Poor knave, I blame thee not, thou art o'er-watch'd. Call Claudius and some other of my men; I'll have them sleep on cushions in my tent.

You sound tired. Poor man, I don't blame you. You have been overworked. Call Claudius and some of the other men to sleep on cushions in my tent.

Lucius

Varro and Claudius!

Varro and Claudius!

Enter Varro and Claudius.

Varro

Calls my lord?

You called, my lord?

Brutus

I pray you, sirs, lie in my tent and sleep; It may be I shall raise you by-and-by On business to my brother Cassius.

Do you mind, sirs, sleeping in here. I may wake up and need you to take a message to my brother, Cassius.

Varro

So please you, we will stand and watch your pleasure.

We will stand guard.

Brutus

I would not have it so; lie down, good sirs: It may be I shall otherwise bethink me.-- Look, Lucius, here's the book I sought for so; I put it in the pocket of my gown.

No, lie down. Look, Lucius, here's the book I was looking for. I put it in the pocket of my gown.

Varro and Claudius lie down.

Lucius

I was sure your lordship did not give it me.

I didn't think you gave it to me.

Brutus

Bear with me, good boy, I am much forgetful. Canst thou hold up thy heavy eyes awhile, And touch thy instrument a strain or two?

Sorry, boy, I am very forgetful. Can you stay awake a little longer and play some music?

Lucius

Ay, my lord, an't please you.

Yes, my lord, if it pleases you.

Brutus

It does, my boy: I trouble thee too much, but thou art willing.

It does, my boy. I know I am a lot of trouble.

Lucius

It is my duty, sir.

It's my duty, sir.

Brutus

I should not urge thy duty past thy might; I know young bloods look for a time of rest.

You need your rest, too. I shouldn't trouble you so much.

Lucius

I have slept, my lord, already.

I have already slept, my lord.

Brutus

It was well done; and thou shalt sleep again; I will not hold thee long: if I do live, I will be good to thee.--

I promise I won't keep you long, and if I do, I'll pay you back.

Music and song.

This is a sleepy tune.--O murderous Slumber, Lay'st thou thy leaden mace upon my boy, That plays thee music?--Gentle knave, good night; I will not do thee so much wrong to wake thee: If thou dost nod, thou breakst thy instrument; I'll take it from thee; and, good boy, good night.-- Let me see, let me see; is not the leaf turn'd down Where I left reading? Here it is, I think.

This is a sleepy tune. Oh, let the music help me sleep. You may go now. You might fall asleep on your instrument. Give it to me and have a good night. Let's see. Where did I leave off? Here is the page, I think.

Enter the Ghost of Caesar.

How ill this taper burns! Ha! who comes here? I think it is the weakness of mine eyes That shapes this monstrous apparition. It comes upon me.--Art thou any thing? Art thou some god, some angel, or some devil, That makest my blood cold and my hair to stare? Speak to me what thou art.

How weird this candle is burning! Who's there? My eyes must be weak; I think I see a ghost. Are you some god, or angel, or devil. You make my blood cold and my hair stand on end. Tell me what you are.

Ghost

Thy evil spirit, Brutus.

I am your evil spirit, Brutus.

Brutus

Why comest thou?

Why are you here?

Ghost

To tell thee thou shalt see me at Philippi.

To tell you I will be in Philippi.

Brutus

Well; then I shall see thee again?

Well, then I will see you again.

Ghost

Ay, at Philippi.

Yes, at Philippi.

Brutus

Why, I will see thee at Philippi, then.

Why will I see you at Philippi?

Exit Ghost.

Now I have taken heart, thou vanishest: Ill spirit, I would hold more talk with thee.-- Boy! Lucius!--Varro! Claudius! Sirs, awake!--Claudius!

Now, that I am curious, you have disappeared. Evil spirit, I would like to talk with you some more. Lucius! Varro! Claudius! Wake up! Claudius!

Lucius

The strings, my lord, are false.

The strings are not right, my lord.

Brutus

He thinks he still is at his instrument.-- Lucius, awake!

He thinks he's still playing his instrument. Wake up, Lucius!

Lucius

My lord?

My lord?

Brutus

Didst thou dream, Lucius, that thou so criedst out?

Did you dream and cry out in your sleep, Lucius?

Lucius

My lord, I do not know that I did cry.

I don't think so.

Brutus

Yes, that thou didst: didst thou see any thing?

You did. Did you see anything?

Lucius

Nothing, my lord.

Nothing, my lord.

Brutus

Sleep again, Lucius.--Sirrah Claudius!-- [To Varro.] Fellow thou, awake!

Go back to sleep, Lucius. Claudius!

To Varro.

Are you awake?

Varro

My lord?

My lord?

Claudius

My lord?

My lord?

Brutus

Why did you so cry out, sirs, in your sleep?

Why did you all cry out in your sleep?

Varro and Claudius

Did we, my lord?

Did we, my lord?

Brutus

Ay: saw you any thing?

Yes, did you see anything?

Varro

No, my lord, I saw nothing.

No, I didn't.

Claudius

Nor I, my lord.

Me either.

Brutus

Go and commend me to my brother Cassius; Bid him set on his powers betimes before, And we will follow.

Go tell Cassius, to set out first thing and we will follow him.

Varro and Claudius

It shall be done, my lord.

We will, my lord.

Exit.

Act V

Scene I: The plains of Philippi.

Enter Octavius, Antony, and their army.

Octavius

Now, Antony, our hopes are answered. You said the enemy would not come down, But keep the hills and upper regions: It proves not so; their battles are at hand: They mean to warn us at Philippi here, Answering before we do demand of them.

Now, Antony, our hopes are answered. You thought the enemy wouldn't come to us, but stay in the hills. Yet, here they are to meet us.

Antony

Tut, I am in their bosoms, and I know Wherefore they do it: they could be content To visit other places; and come down With fearful bravery, thinking by this face To fasten in our thoughts that they have courage; But 'tis not so.

I know them, and I know what they are up to. They want us to think they are brave, but I know better.

Enter a Messenger.

Messenger

Prepare you, generals: The enemy comes on in gallant show; Their bloody sign of battle is hung out, And something to be done immediately.

Get ready, generals, the enemy is coming. Their battle sign is out and something needs to be done immediately.

Antony

Octavius, lead your battle softly on, Upon the left hand of the even field.

Octavius, lead your men on the left side of the field.

Octavius

Upon the right hand I; keep thou the left.

I'll take the right. You take the left.

Antony

Why do you cross me in this exigent?

Why do you disagree with me in this dire hour?

Octavius

I do not cross you; but I will do so.

I'm not disagreeing with you, but I will.

March.

Drum. Enter Brutus, Cassius, and their armies. Lucilius, Titinius, Messalus, and others.

Brutus

They stand, and would have parley.

They stand and are ready to fight.

Cassius

Stand fast, Titinius: we must out and talk.

Stay here, Titinius. We must ride out and talk.

Octavius

Mark Antony, shall we give sign of battle?

Mark Antony, shall we give sign of battle?

Antony

No, Caesar, we will answer on their charge. Make forth; the generals would have some words.

No, Caesar, we wait until they charge. Go forward. The generals want to talk.

Octavius

Stir not until the signal.

Don't do anything until I give you the signal.

Brutus

Words before blows: is it so, countrymen?

Words before blows. So, that's how it's going to be, countrymen.

Octavius

Not that we love words better, as you do.

We don't love words like you do.

Brutus

Good words are better than bad strokes, Octavius.

Good words are better than bad fighting, Octavius.

Antony

In your bad strokes, Brutus, you give good words: Witness the hole you made in Caesar's heart, Crying, "Long live! Hail, Caesar!"

You have good words for your bad deeds. Weren't you crying out, "Hail, Caesar," when you were stabbing him?

Cassius

Antony, The posture of your blows are yet unknown; But for your words, they rob the Hybla bees, And leave them honeyless.

Antony, we don't know how well you fight, but your words drip with honey.

Antony

Not stingless too.

They don't sting, though.

Brutus

O, yes, and soundless too, For you have stol'n their buzzing, Antony, And very wisely threat before you sting.

Your words are not soundless, either. They are very effective, Antony, warning your enemy before you fight.

Antony

Villains, you did not so when your vile daggers Hack'd one another in the sides of Caesar: You show'd your teeth like apes, and fawn'd like hounds, And bow'd like bondmen, kissing Caesar's feet; Whilst damned Casca, like a cur, behind Struck Caesar on the neck. O flatterers!

That's better than what you did when you acted like beasts and killed Caesar, stabbing him in his sides, while Casca struck from behind, you flatterers.

Cassius

Flatterers!--Now, Brutus, thank yourself: This tongue had not offended so to-day, If Cassius might have ruled.

Flatterers! We wouldn't be here were I the ruler.

Octavius

Come, come, the cause: if arguing makes us sweat, The proof of it will turn to redder drops. Look,-- I draw a sword against conspirators: When think you that the sword goes up again? Never, till Caesar's three and thirty wounds Be well avenged; or till another Caesar Have added slaughter to the sword of traitors.

Come on, get to the point. We aren't here to argue. I draw my sword against conspirators and keep it up until Caesar's death is avenged, or until I have been killed by the same traitors.

Brutus

Caesar, thou canst not die by traitors' hands, Unless thou bring'st them with thee.

You aren't going to die at the hands of a traitor, unless you kill yourself.

Octavius

So I hope; I was not born to die on Brutus' sword.

That's my hope. I was not born to die on Brutus's sword.

Brutus

O, if thou wert the noblest of thy strain, Young man, thou couldst not die more honourably.

You couldn't die a more honorable death.

Cassius

A peevish school boy, worthless of such honour, Join'd with a masker and a reveller!

You are just a school boy and not worthy of such an honor.

Antony

Old Cassius still!

There's the old Cassius!

Octavius

Come, Antony; away!-- Defiance, traitors, hurl we in your teeth: If you dare fight today, come to the field; If not, when you have stomachs.

Come on, Antony. Let's go! Traitors, if you dare to fight today, come to the field. If not, come when you have the stomachs for it.

Exit Octavius, Antony, and their armies.

Cassius

Why, now, blow wind, swell billow, and swim bark! The storm is up, and all is on the hazard.

Why now are we having a storm?

Brutus

Ho, Lucilius! Hark, a word with you.

Hey, Lucilius! Listen, I need a word with you.

Lucilius

Standing forward.

My lord?

I'm listening.

CASSIUS

Messala,--

MESSALA

What says my General?

Cassius

Messala, This is my birth-day; as this very day Was Cassius born. Give me thy hand, Messala: Be thou my witness that against my will, As Pompey was, am I compell'd to set Upon one battle all our liberties. You know that I held Epicurus strong, And his opinion: now I change my mind, And partly credit things that do presage. Coming from Sardis, on our former ensign Two mighty eagles fell; and there they perch'd, Gorging and feeding from our soldiers' hands; Who to Philippi here consorted us: This morning are they fled away and gone; And in their steads do ravens, crows, and kites Fly o'er our heads and downward look on us, As we were sickly prey: their shadows seem A canopy most fatal, under which Our army lies, ready to give up the ghost.

Messala, this is my birthday. Give me your hand and be my witness that I am here against my will. I am going to set all of our freedom on the line. You know that believed in Epicurus, but now I have changed my mind. On the way from Sardis, I saw two mighty eagles fall and feed from our soldiers' hands. They are gone, now, and ravens and crows circle us like we are about to be prey. We seem ready to die.

Messala

Believe not so.

I don't think so.

Cassius

I but believe it partly; For I am fresh of spirit, and resolved To meet all perils very constantly.

I believe it partly, because I am ready.

Brutus

Even so, Lucilius.

Even so, Lucilius.

Cassius

Now, most noble Brutus, The gods to-day stand friendly, that we may, Lovers in peace, lead on our days to age! But, since th' affairs of men rest still incertain, Let's reason with the worst that may befall. If we do lose this battle, then is this The very last time we shall speak together: What are you then determined to do?

Now, most noble Brutus, the gods are going to be friendly today so we lovers of peace may live to a ripe old age. But, since we are still unsure how this is going to turn out let's just say we lose today. What are you going to do then?

Brutus

Even by the rule of that philosophy By which I did blame Cato for the death Which he did give himself;--I know not how, But I do find it cowardly and vile, For fear of what might fall, so to prevent The time of life;--arming myself with patience To stay the providence of some high powers That govern us below.

I am going to stay the course with patience, unlike Cato who killed himself for fear of the unknown.

Cassius

Then, if we lose this battle, You are contented to be led in triumph Thorough the streets of Rome?

Then, if we lose, you are going to be content to be led through the streets of Rome?

Brutus

No, Cassius, no: think not, thou noble Roman, That ever Brutus will go bound to Rome; He bears too great a mind. But this same day Must end that work the Ides of March begun; And whether we shall meet again I know not. Therefore our everlasting farewell take: For ever, and for ever, farewell, Cassius! If we do meet again, why, we shall smile; If not, why, then this parting was well made.

No, Cassius, I don't think so. Any Roman who thinks I will go into Rome in handcuffs thinks too much of himself. Today, we will finish what was started on March 15th. I don't know if we will meet again, so let's say our goodbyes. Farewell, Cassius! If we do meet again, let's smile, and know we parted well.

Cassius

For ever and for ever farewell, Brutus! If we do meet again, we'll smile indeed; If not, 'tis true this parting was well made.

If we meet again, Brutus, we will smile, indeed. If not, we did part well.

Brutus

Why then, lead on. O, that a man might know The end of this day's business ere it come! But it sufficeth that the day will end, And then the end is known.--Come, ho! away!

Well, then, let's go. I wish I knew what is about to happen, but the day will end all the same and then, I'll know. Let's go!

Exit.

Scene II: The same field of battle.

Alarm. Enter Brutus and Messala.

Brutus

Ride, ride, Messala, ride, and give these bills Unto the legions on the other side: Let them set on at once; for I perceive But cold demeanor in Octavius' wing, And sudden push gives them the overthrow. Ride, ride, Messala: let them all come down.

Ride, ride, Messala, and give these orders to the men on the other side.

Loud alarm.

Let them start at once, because I believe Octavius's men are not ready. Hurry, Messala, ride. Let them all come down.

Exit.

Scene III: Another part of the field.

Alarms. Enter Cassius and Titinius.

Cassius

O, look, Titinius, look, the villains fly! Myself have to mine own turn'd enemy: This ensign here of mine was turning back; I slew the coward, and did take it from him.

Oh, look, Titinius. Look, the enemy is fleeing! One of my men tried to turn back, but I killed him.

Titinius

O Cassius, Brutus gave the word too early; Who, having some advantage on Octavius, Took it too eagerly: his soldiers fell to spoil, Whilst we by Antony are all enclosed.

Oh, Cassius, Brutus gave the word too early. He thought he had advantage over Octavius, but he was too eager. His soldiers have started looting, and we're surrounded by Antony.

Pindarus

Fly further off, my lord, fly further off; Mark Antony is in your tents, my lord: Fly, therefore, noble Cassius, fly far' off.

You must flee, my lord, go away. Mark Antony is in your tents, my lord. You must leave.

Cassius

This hill is far enough.--Look, look, Titinius; Are those my tents where I perceive the fire?

I will go to the hills. Are those my tents over there where I see fire?

Titinius

They are, my lord.

They are, my lord.

Cassius

Titinius, if thou lovest me, Mount thou my horse and hide thy spurs in him, Till he have brought thee up to yonder troops And here again; that I may rest assured Whether yond troops are friend or enemy.

Titinius, if you love me, get on my horse and spur him until he has taken you up to the troops and back again, so I may know if the troops are friend or enemy.

Titinius

I will be here again, even with a thought.

I will be right back.

Exit.

Cassius

Go, Pindarus, get higher on that hill: My sight was ever thick: regard Titinius, And tell me what thou notest about the field.--

Pindarus, get higher on that hill and watch Titinius. Tell me what you see on the battlefield.

Pindarus ascends the hill.

This day I breathed first: time is come round, And where I did begin, there shall I end; My life is run his compass.--Sirrah, what news?

This is the first and last day I will breathe. My life has run its course. What news, sir?

Pindarus

Above.

O my lord!

Oh, my lord!

Cassius

What news?

What is it?

Pindarus

Above.

Titinius is enclosed round about With horsemen, that make to him on the spur: Yet he spurs on. Now they are almost on him.-- Now, Titinius!--Now some 'light. O, he 'lights too: He's ta'en; [Shout.] and, hark! they shout for joy.

Titinius is surrounded by men who are chasing him. They are almost on him. Now, Titinius is getting down. They have taken him.

Shout!

They are shouting for joy.

Cassius

Come down; behold no more.-- O, coward that I am, to live so long, To see my best friend ta'en before my face!

Come down. Don't look anymore. Oh, I am such a coward to watch my best friend be taken before my eyes!

Pindarus descends.

Come hither, sirrah: In Parthia did I take thee prisoner; And then I swore thee, saving of thy life, That whatsoever I did bid thee do, Thou shouldst attempt it. Come now, keep thine oath; Now be a freeman; and with this good sword, That ran through Caesar's bowels, search this bosom. Stand not to answer: here, take thou the hilts; And when my face is cover'd, as 'tis now, Guide thou the sword.--Caesar, thou art revenged, Even with the sword that kill'd thee.

Come here, sir. I took you prisoner in Parthia, and I swore after I saved your life you had to do whatever I asked. It's time to keep that oath. Be a freeman and with this sword that killed Caesar, stab me in the heart. Don't stand there. Take it, and when my face is covered, do it.

Pindarus stabs him.

Caesar, you are revenged with the sword that killed you.

Dies.

Pindarus

So, I am free, yet would not so have been, Durst I have done my will.--O Cassius! Far from this country Pindarus shall run, Where never Roman shall take note of him.

So, I am free, but I wouldn't be if I had way. Oh, Cassius, I am going to run far from here where no Roman can find me.

Exit.

Re-enter Titinius with Messala.

Messala

It is but change, Titinius; for Octavius Is overthrown by noble Brutus' power, As Cassius' legions are by Antony.

Octavius is overthrown and Antony took Cassius's men.

Titinius

These tidings would well comfort Cassius.

Cassius will be comforted by this message.

Messala

Where did you leave him?

Where did you leave him?

Titinius

All disconsolate, With Pindarus his bondman, on this hill.

He was here on this hill with his slave, Pindarus.

Messala

Is not that he that lies upon the ground?

Isn't that him on the ground?

Titinius

He lies not like the living. O my heart!

He doesn't look alive. Oh, my heart!

Messala

Is not that he?

Isn't that him?

Titinius

No, this was he, Messala, But Cassius is no more.--O setting Sun, As in thy red rays thou dost sink to night, So in his red blood Cassius' day is set, The sun of Rome is set! Our day is gone; Clouds, dews, and dangers come; our deeds are done! Mistrust of my success hath done this deed.

Yes, this is him, Messala. Cassius's life is over like the setting sun, spreading its red light over the earth. Our day is gone and our deeds are done. He didn't believe I would make it.

Messala

Mistrust of good success hath done this deed. O hateful Error, Melancholy's child! Why dost thou show to the apt thoughts of men The things that are not? O Error, soon conceived, Thou never comest unto a happy birth, But kill'st the mother that engender'd thee!

He didn't think you would succeed and his error has cost him his life. Why do men always imagine the worst?

Titinius

What, Pindarus! where art thou, Pindarus?

Where is Pindarus? Pindarus!

Messala

Seek him, Titinius, whilst I go to meet The noble Brutus, thrusting this report Into his ears: I may say, thrusting it; For piercing steel and darts envenomed Shall be as welcome to the ears of Brutus As tidings of this sight.

Look for him, Titinius, while I go meet Brutus and tell him what has happened. Brutus is not going to like hearing this.

Titinius

Hie you, Messala, And I will seek for Pindarus the while.--

Hurry, Messala, and I will look for Pindarus.

Exit Messala.

Why didst thou send me forth, brave Cassius? Did I not meet thy friends? And did not they Put on my brows this wreath of victory, And bid me give it thee? Didst thou not hear their shouts? Alas, thou hast misconstrued every thing! But, hold thee, take this garland on thy brow; Thy Brutus bid me give it thee, and I Will do his bidding.-- Brutus, come apace, And see how I regarded Caius Cassius.-- By your leave, gods: this is a Roman's part: Come, Cassius' sword, and find Titinius' heart.

Why did you send me, brave Cassius? Didn't I meet your friends who gave me this wreath of victory to give to you? Didn't you hear the cheering? You misunderstood everything! But, take this wreath and wear it like Brutus wanted, so he can see I followed orders. Now, by the gods, I am taking your sword to find my heart.

Kills himself.

Alarms. Re-enter Messala with Brutus, Cato, Strato, Volumnius and Lucilius.

Brutus

Where, where, Messala, doth his body lie?

Where, Messala, is his body?

Messala

Lo, yonder, and Titinius mourning it.

Over there, with Titinius mourning over it.

Brutus

Titinius' face is upward.

Titinius is lying face up.

Cato

He is slain.

He is dead.

Brutus

O Julius Caesar, thou art mighty yet! Thy spirit walks abroad, and turns our swords In our own proper entrails.

Oh, Julius Caesar, you are still mighty! Your spirit walks around and turns our swords against us.

Low alarms.

Cato

Brave Titinius! Look whether he have not crown'd dead Cassius!

Brave Titinius! See if he crowned Cassius.

Brutus

Are yet two Romans living such as these?-- The last of all the Romans, fare thee well! It is impossible that ever Rome Should breed thy fellow.--Friends, I owe more tears To this dead man than you shall see me pay.-- I shall find time, Cassius, I shall find time.-- Come therefore, and to Thassos send his body: His funerals shall not be in our camp, Lest it discomfort us.--Lucilius, come;-- And come, young Cato;--let us to the field.-- Labeo and Flavius, set our battles on:-- 'Tis three o'clock; and Romans, yet ere night We shall try fortune in a second fight.

Are there two Romans alive like these? They were the last of their kind. Friends, I should cry, but I will not. Cassius, I will find time to mourn you. Send his body to Thasos for the funeral. We don't want to have it in the camp. Lucilius and young Cato, let's go back to the battlefield. Laveo and Flavius get ready to fight. We will try a second time to triumph.

Exit.

Scene IV: Another part of the field.

Alarm. Enter fighting soldiers of both armies, then Brutus, Cato, Lucilius, and others.

Brutus

Yet, countrymen, O, yet hold up your heads!

Hold up your heads, countrymen! Don't give up!

Cato

What bastard doth not? Who will go with me? I will proclaim my name about the field:-- I am the son of Marcus Cato, ho! A foe to tyrants, and my country's friend; I am the son of Marcus Cato, ho!

What bastard is not? Who will go with me? I will proclaim my name about the field. I am the son of Marcus Cato, a foe to tyrants and a friend to Rome. I am the son of Marcus Cato!

Brutus

And I am Brutus, Marcus Brutus, I; Brutus, my country's friend; know me for Brutus!

And I am Brutus, Marcus Brutus. I am my country's friend. You know me!

Exit.

Lucilius

O young and noble Cato, art thou down? Why, now thou diest as bravely as Titinius; And mayst be honour'd, being Cato's son.

Oh, young and noble Cato, are you hurt? You have died as bravely as Titinius and will be honored as Cato's son.

First Soldier

Yield, or thou diest.

We must give up or die.

Lucilius

Only I yield to die: There is so much that thou wilt kill me straight; [Offering money.] Kill Brutus, and be honour'd in his death.

I will only give up to death.

Offering money.

Kill Brutus, and be honored for his death.

First Soldier

We must not. A noble prisoner!

We can't. He is a noble prisoner!

Second Soldier

Room, ho! Tell Antony, Brutus is ta'en.

Make way! Tell Antony, Brutus has been captured.

First Soldier

I'll tell the news. Here comes the General.--

I'll tell him. Here comes the general.

Enter Antony.

Brutus is ta'en, Brutus is ta'en, my lord.

Antony

Where is he?

Where is he?

Lucilius

Safe, Antony; Brutus is safe enough: I dare assure thee that no enemy Shall ever take alive the noble
Brutus: The gods defend him from so great a shame! When you do find him, or alive or dead, He will be found
like Brutus, like himself.

*He is safe enough, Antony. I assure you no enemy will take him alive. The gods defend him from such a great
shame! When you do find him, he will be Brutus, alive or dead.*

Antony

This is not Brutus, friend; but, I assure you, A prize no less in worth. Keep this man safe, Give him all kindness;
I had rather have Such men my friends than enemies. Go on, And see whether Brutus be alive or dead; And
bring us word unto Octavius' tent How everything is chanced.

*This is not Brutus, friend, but I assure you it is a prize, nevertheless. Keep this man safe. Treat him with kindness.
I had rather have such men as my friends than my enemies. Go on, and see if Brutus is alive or dead, and come
tell us in Octavius's tent.*

Exit.

Scene V: Another part of the field.

Enter Brutus, Dardanius, Clitus, Strato, and Volumnius.

Brutus

Come, poor remains of friends, rest on this rock.

Come on, friends. Let's rest on this rock.

Clitus

Statilius show'd the torch-light; but, my lord, He came not back: he is or ta'en or slain.

Statilius showed the torch was lit, but he never came back. He is either captured or dead.

Brutus

Sit thee down, Clitus: slaying is the word; It is a deed in fashion. Hark thee, Clitus.

Sit down, Clitus. He is probably dead. Listen.

Whispers.

Clitus

What, I, my lord? No, not for all the world.

No, not me lord. Not for all of the world.

Brutus

Peace then! no words.

Be quiet, then.

Clitus

I'll rather kill myself.

I'd rather kill myself.

Brutus

Hark thee, Dardanius.

Listen, Dardanius.

Whispers.

Dardanius

Shall I do such a deed?

Would I do such a deed?

Clitus

O Dardanius!

Oh, Dardanius!

Dardanius

O Clitus!

Oh, Clitus!

Clitus

What ill request did Brutus make to thee?

What did Brutus ask of you?

Dardanius

To kill him, Clitus. Look, he meditates.

He wants me to kill him. Look, he's thinking about it.

Clitus

Now is that noble vessel full of grief, That it runs over even at his eyes.

He is so full of grief, it is running over in his eyes.

Brutus

Come hither, good Volumnius; list a word.

Come here, Volumnius. I need a word with you.

Volumnius

What says my lord?

What do you need, my lord?

Brutus

Why, this, Volumnius: The ghost of Caesar hath appear'd to me Two several times by night; at Sardis once, And this last night here in Philippi fields: I know my hour is come.

The ghost of Caesar has appeared to me twice by night, once in Sardis and last night in Philippi. I know my time has come.

Volumnius

Not so, my lord.

You don't know that, my lord.

Brutus

Nay I am sure it is, Volumnius. Thou seest the world, Volumnius, how it goes; Our enemies have beat us to the pit:

No, I am sure of it, Volumnius. Our enemies have beaten us. I know what's coming next.

Low alarms.

It is more worthy to leap in ourselves Than tarry till they push us. Good Volumnius, Thou know'st that we two went to school together; Even for that our love of old, I pr'ythee, Hold thou my sword-hilts, whilst I run on it.

It is better to off ourselves than have them do it. Volumnius, you know we went to school together. We go back a long way. Please, hold my sword, so I may run into it.

Volumnius

That's not an office for a friend, my lord.

That's not something a friend can do, my lord.

Alarm.

Clitus

Fly, fly, my lord! there is no tarrying here.

Run, run, my lord. You can't sit here.

Brutus

Farewell to you;--and you;--and you, Volumnius.-- Strato, thou hast been all this while asleep; Farewell to thee too, Strato.--Countrymen, My heart doth joy, that yet in all my life I found no man but he was true to me. I shall have glory by this losing day, More than Octavius and Mark Antony By this vile conquest shall attain unto. So, fare you well at once; for Brutus' tongue Hath almost ended his life's history: Night hangs upon mine eyes; my bones would rest That have but labour'd to attain this hour.

Farewell my friends. Goodbye, Strato. My heart is full of joy that in all of my life, I never met an untrue man. I will have triumph greater than Octavius and Mark Antony today. So, goodbye once and for all. It's my time to rest.

Alarm. Cries to run from within.

Clitus

Fly, my lord, fly!

Run, my lord, run.

Brutus

Hence! I will follow.--

Go. I will follow.

Exit Clitus, Dardanius, and Volumnius.

I pr'ythee, Strato, stay thou by thy lord: Thou art a fellow of a good respect; Thy life hath had some smack of honor in it: Hold, then, my sword, and turn away thy face, While I do run upon it. Wilt thou, Strato?

I pray you will help me, Strato. You are respectful fellow, and your life has been honorable. Hold my sword and turn your eyes away. Will you, Strato?

Strato

Give me your hand first: fare you well, my lord.

Give me your hand first. Goodbye, my lord.

Brutus

Farewell, good Strato.--Caesar, now be still: I kill'd not thee with half so good a will.

Goodbye, Strato.

Runs on his sword.

Caesar, you may rest. I wanted to kill myself more than you.

Dies.

Alarm. Retreat. Enter Octavius, Antony, Messala, Lucilius, and the army.

Octavius

What man is that?

Who is that man?

Messala

My master's man.--Strato, where is thy master?

My master's man. Strato, where is your master?

Strato

Free from the bondage you are in, Messala: The conquerors can but make a fire of him; For Brutus only overcame himself, And no man else hath honour by his death.

He is free from the bondage you are in, Messala. The conquerors can burn him, but they can't kill him, so no man can claim honor by his death.

Lucilius

So Brutus should be found.--I thank thee, Brutus, That thou hast proved Lucilius' saying true.

So, Brutus should be found. Thank you, Brutus, for proving me right.

Octavius

All that served Brutus, I will entertain them.-- Fellow, wilt thou bestow thy time with me?

All that served Brutus will be entertained. Will you give me your time?

Strato

Ay, if Messala will prefer me to you.

Yes, if Messala will prefer me to you.

Octavius

Do so, good Messala.

Do so, Messala.

Messala

How died my master, Strato?

How did my master die, Strato?

Strato

I held the sword, and he did run on it.

I held the sword and he ran upon it.

Messala

Octavius, then take him to follow thee, That did the latest service to my master.

You may have him, Octavius, for his service to my master.

Antony

This was the noblest Roman of them all: All the conspirators, save only he, Did that they did in envy of great Caesar; He only, in a general-honest thought And common good to all, made one of them. His life was gentle; and the elements So mix'd in him that Nature might stand up And say to all the world, "This was a man!"

This was the noblest Roman of them all. All the conspirators did what they did out of envy, except for him. He was the only one who thought his actions were for the common good to his country. He lived a gentle life, so that Nature would say, "That was a man!"

Octavius

According to his virtue let us use him With all respect and rites of burial. Within my tent his bones to-night shall lie, Most like a soldier, order'd honorably.-- So, call the field to rest; and let's away, To part the glories of this happy day.

Let's honor his life and put his body in my tent. Call the field to rest and let's go away to celebrate this happy day.

Exit.

THE END

About BookCaps

We all need refreshers every now and then. Whether you are a student trying to cram for that big final, or someone just trying to understand a book more, BookCaps can help. We are a small, but growing company, and are adding titles every month.

Visit www.bookcaps.com to see more of our books, or contact us with any questions.

Printed in Great Britain
by Amazon

13775058R00127